Dr Lynda Foulder-Hughes is a consultant psychotherapist. She was one of the youngest allied health professionals in the UK to hold both a PhD and a master's degree. She has worked in hospitals, clinics, community settings, education and television.

Her pioneering work has resulted in some high-profile awards and recognitions during her 30-year career; including in 2015 being named as one of Newsweek Magazine's "21st Century Professionals" across two editions. Lynda also worked for the BBC, where she acted as the specialist series consultant on the twice BAFTA nominated children's television series, *Tree Fu Tom*. She is credited on every episode of show, which is screened in over 120 countries globally.

Alongside her clinical work, Lynda has published her research in many high impact international publications. Her seminal work on helping adult survivors of childhood sexual abuse was published in 1998 and continues to be an influential piece of writing.

Lynda takes a highly empathetic approach with each person she works with. In her personal life, she has overcome some massive challenges. She was born into a deprived Liverpool family to a single teen-aged mother in 1968. She had a tough upbringing and left home aged just 17. Few people with Lynda's childhood go onto achieve the success or qualifications which she has. She is living proof that you can succeed in life no matter what.

Remind is her first book. It is a holistic self-help model based on research, traditional evidenced-based therapies, alongside metaphysical, transpersonal, and positive psychology approaches, combined with her 30 years of professional experience.

This book is dedicated to my husband John and our children
Sam, Isobel, and Luke.

Also, to:

Ruth and Bob Williams

Dave Foy

Peter and Joan Finnigan

Joe Musker

Lynda Parry

Dr Lynda Foulder-Hughes

REMIND

The Prescription for
Happiness, Success, and
Fulfilment in Life

AUSTIN MACAULEY PUBLISHERS™

LONDON • CAMBRIDGE • NEW YORK • SHARJAH

A CIP catalogue record for this title is available from the British Library.

ISBN 9781398490086 (Paperback)
ISBN 9781398490093 (ePub e-book)

www.austinmacauley.com

First Published 2023
Austin Macauley Publishers Ltd®
1 Canada Square
Canary Wharf
London
E14 5AA

20230322

Table of Contents

Introduction: The Remind Approach   9

Chapter 1: R = Routine   11

Chapter 2: E = Exercise   31

Chapter 3: M = Mindfulness   51

Chapter 4: I = Invest in Self and Others – Self   83

Chapter 5: I = Invest in Self and Others – Others   116

Chapter 6: N = Nature   134

Chapter 7: D = Diet   144

Chapter 8: REMIND Approach in Action   159

Chapter 9: Asking for Help   178

Bibliography   182

Introduction
The Remind Approach

The REMIND approach can be used to help you to achieve your goals, solve problems, address past difficulties and to move into the future in a positive and hopeful way. Focusing on what is proven to work, it combines both traditional evidenced-based therapy, with metaphysical and transpersonal approaches. It is a holistic model that was developed alongside Dr Lynda Foulder-Hughes's own 30 years' therapy and research experience. It is a truly unique self-help framework that will change your life forever.

The REMIND approach combines daily routine, exercise, mindfulness, investing in self and others, nature, and diet in a focused way. Powerful affirmations are incorporated throughout. All these components are seamlessly blended into an easy, workable and effective model, that you can start implementing immediately.

Each chapter explains the separate components of REMIND and how these are all interconnected and dependent upon the other. Throughout the book there are practical activities and case studies designed to both guide and inspire you on your own journey.

Incorporating the REMIND approach will easily provide the tools you need to make the necessary changes right now, to recover from past trauma, and to achieve the enjoyable and successful life you have always dreamt of having.

REMIND really is the prescription for happiness, success, and fulfilment in life.

Chapter 1
R = Routine

'There are only two ways to live your life. One is as
though nothing is a miracle. The other is as though
everything is a miracle.'
(Albert Einstein)

The first concept in the REMIND approach is routine.
Routine is vital to our mental and emotional wellbeing. The
"familiar" feels safe. We crave order in our lives so that we
can feel secure in all we do and all we are. In short, routine in
our lives creates safety. Therefore, routine is a vital
underpinning part of the REMIND approach. This chapter
will introduce you to the concept of establishing a routine and
why having one is extremely beneficial to psychological,
physical, and emotional health.

Why Routine Matters

If we consider the major, well documented life-stressors,
ranging from serious illness, unemployment, to death of a
close family member or friend etc., all share one common
feature: loss of routine. Your life is not just thrown into

emotional chaos by life's major stressors but there will also have been a massive shift in the predictable daily routine you undertake. When we are faced with a significant life event, then it thrusts us immediately back into the primitive "fight or flight response." This then sends a signal to the brain that something has changed in our immediate environment, and we need to be alert. In other words, we are programmed to face imminent danger. It makes us feel like we have lost control and it is this aspect that a routine can help us to restore. So, what I find as a therapist, no matter what difficulty a person presents with, keeping a regular routine is vital for mental survival. The above quotation by Albert Einstein is an excellent one in terms of how you start every day and the approach you take psychologically to it. You can apply the concept of everything within your daily routine as being miraculous, rather than just the mundane.

During the recent global Covid pandemic, what every person had in common, was the fact that their daily lives had changed. So, their routine and sense of safety had been disturbed. Yes, there was a real threat in terms of the virus and the unpredictable nature of its transmission but what most people had lost was control over their own lives. Most of us had to adapt to an ever-changing world and a major shift in our regular, predictable daily routine including, work, education, caring commitments, social life, leisure etc. It was not then surprising that many mental health professionals (myself included) experienced a ten-fold increase in demand for our services.

Having a basic daily routine helps us to build a sense of direction and structure into our daily lives. A regular routine adds both purpose and meaning to our day. Having a routine helps us to establish our place in the world and where we fit in. It is often such a basic (yet over-looked) key component of a person's sense of self and wellbeing, that I am surprised there is not more emphasis placed upon it in the multitude of self-help books available. It makes the "everyday" appear normal and helps restore a sense of calm amongst uncertainty.

Without routine, chaos, anxiety, and depression can ensue. A regular routine promotes a sense of safety and security. This may sound like a very basic description, and yes, often it can be just that simple for many people. When a regular "safe" routine is disturbed, it can literally create a real sense of both chaos and danger in a person's brain. Without a regular structure, that holds both purpose and meaning, then our thoughts are driven inwards, and we begin to ruminate. An article by Ash Fisher published in 2020, stated the importance of how a regular routine can be beneficial to managing both depression and pain. Both physical pain and symptoms of depression can worsen during times of stress and when routine has been disturbed.

As humans we crave safety and security. A regular routine provides both. Anxiety can clearly worsen considerably when a regular routine has been changed. At a basic level we feel out of control and fearful of what may happen. In fact, there is a common saying, "Depression is a condition of the past and anxiety is a condition of the future." This means that thinking and dwelling upon past negative events can keep us trapped in a negative mind set. However, dwelling upon and being fearful about an uncertain future can keep us trapped in an anxious and worried state. Therefore, the safety of a predictable and stable daily routine can help immensely with the uncertainty of an unpredictable future or a sudden traumatic life event.

Interestingly, the importance of routine was raised by Sir Bradley Wiggins in a recent interview in 2022, in the magazine "Men's Health." During the interview the highly decorated Olympic Cyclist and Tour de France winner disclosed his own mental health difficulties and traumatic events from his early life. What was interesting is how important a structured routine is to Sir Bradley in order for him to stay mentally well.

Routine is a vital underpinning component to staying mentally well. There is a clear link between what we expect to happen in certain situations and what will happen. We need to know what to expect from life daily. When we lose control over our lives it causes distress; it is an in-escapable fact. So, we need to feel a sense of safety and comfort from having a routine that we can control.

We may not be able to control the wider, events around the world in terms of Covid, war, famine etc., but we can re-claim our sense of order through routine during any time of personal or wider crisis. It is therefore an essential component to staying mentally well during uncertain times.

The trick is to consider what you can control, not what you cannot.

SMART Goals and Routine

So here we can draw on some of the techniques used regularly in cognitive behavioural therapy (CBT). One technique which links to routine, is often referred to as

SMART goals. It is an acronym, which is commonly attributed to business rather than therapy but has been absorbed as an approach that actually works and is used regularly in CBT. The SMART acronym was first coined in 1981 in the USA by George T. Doran (Doran, 1981).

This stands for: Specific, Measurable, Achievable, Relevant, Time bound.

S = Specific

It is vital to be very specific about what you want to achieve. Do not set a goal that is rather vague. This is a common mistake that many people make, when trying to establish a routine and build in regular goals. So, I often hear examples like, "I want to do more in the day" as a "specific" goal. However, this is not specific enough, it is somewhat vague. A more specific goal example might be, "I want to be able to take a regular walk of 15 minutes each day." As you can see this is a very specific goal, rather than saying, "I want to do more in the day." So, be specific at the start.

M = Measurable

For something to be measurable it must have a starting point and an end point. The importance of it being specific in nature links in very closely to it being measurable. That way you can see how well you are progressing. It builds into a sense of mastery. So, when we "master" a skill (in anything) this directly impacts into our sense of self-efficacy (how well we can do things) and this can affect our self-esteem in a positive way. They also need to be meaningful to you and your individual circumstances. All activity and goals should be both purposeful and meaningful in their nature, as this keeps you motivated. How well a person is motivated to succeed is also a key determinant of success. Motivated people generally feel better about themselves than those who lack motivation. Therefore, in setting goals, make sure they hold a personal meaning for you and can be measured. That way you will be driven to continue. In other words, make the goal something you will enjoy so it holds meaning for you.

A = Achievable

There is absolutely no point in setting a goal that you know you will not achieve. Do not set yourself up for failure if you want to feel better and stick to a regular routine. Breaking the steps of the goal down into small achievable ones will instil a sense of accomplishment. So, if your overall goal is to be able to take a regular daily 15-minute walk outside, then start with a shorter five minute walk (we will discuss the five minute rule later and its importance in therapy). In starting with goals that are achievable, you are promoting a more positive outlook towards the future. It is certainly not about taking the "easy way" but the small steps you make at the start will allow you to make the "giant strides" later. If you have always harboured the dream of going to university and gaining a degree but you do not have any qualifications to get in, then look at the steps you need to take. Plan carefully the steps you need to take to make your goal achievable. Again, break down each part of your end goal into small achievable steps so that each mini goal is achievable, and you do not give up.

R = Relevant

These goals also need to be realistic. There is no point in setting a goal which is neither relevant to yourself nor realistic to achieve. Setting an impossible goal which holds no relevance to yourself will not result in you achieving it. The goal needs to interest you in the first place and hold some personal relevance to you. You may have always harboured a dream of climbing Mount Everest. However, you would not set the goal of climbing Mount Everest tomorrow if you have never even climbed a local hill, let alone a mountain. This may seem like an extreme example, but it is a way of looking at how relevant your goals are to your own personal setting. However, if we take the example of taking the regular 15-minute walk each day and being able to make it part of your regular daily routine, it is both relevant and realistic.

T = Time Bound

If you want to achieve a goal and build it into to your regular routine, then you need to set a time frame in which to achieve it. Taking the smaller steps, and the example of the walking, is a good one of a goal which can be set within a realistic time frame. You can easily set achievable weekly goals to make them time bound.

Also, in setting goals you need to consider one vital component: How cost effective is it? Can you afford to achieve your goal and build it into your daily routine? So, for example, if one of your goals is to take up a daily horse ride but you cannot afford the funds to take up horse riding then no matter how you structure your time, you will not achieve your goal. So, when setting a realistic time frame to build your goals into your regular routine, make sure they can be achieved by ensuring you have any necessary funds in place. Build in the small steps that lead towards you being able to afford that "horse"! Otherwise, goals will not be achievable.

Importance of a Regular Routine:
Four-step Morning Routine.

'Conquer the morning and you will seize the day.'

The morning is often the time of day that many people find the most challenging. The above quotation can act almost as a mantra for motivation. Some of the people I work with have it written down next to their beds, so it is the first thing they see when they wake up. The morning is the most important time of the day, as it signifies a "fresh start" and a vehicle for both hope and optimism. It does not have to signify despair and negativity. We can change for the better. The trick is to establish a predictable and safe routine that we can control. Indeed, a routine which will set us up for an optimistic day ahead.

At a basic level I ask my own clients to do the following four step morning routine procedure. I developed this simple four step routine as it is easy to follow and stick to. It helps to establish a regular, daily, morning schedule, which is specific, achievable, realistic and time bound. Therefore, it contains all the elements of a SMART goal structure.

As a therapist, I know from my patients and clients, that when they feel low in mood all the steps involved in the SMART goals can feel like impossible and overwhelming tasks to achieve. It really helps to have an order and a routine to regularly base your day on. Having the following framework is an excellent way of gaining control each day and improving mood (even if you have early morning waking associated with depression).

1) **Go to bed and get up at the same time each day.**

A regular sleep and waking routine are vital for mental wellbeing. When people lack a structured routine one thing that always stands out to me as a therapist is their ability to establish a structured bedtime habit. Sleep is nearly always impacted upon when mood is low. We know that people who suffer from anxiety or depression (or both together) have difficulties with restful sleep and routine. They may sleep too much or not enough. Mood and sleep are inextricably linked.

As part of a CBT approach, I use a sleep restriction method to treat difficulties with my own patients. The sleep restriction method was originally developed by Dr Arthur J Spielman an American psychologist who first identified the link between restricting the amount of time spent in bed and how it could lead to establishing improved sleeping patters (Spielman et al.,1987). This approach has now been absorbed into CBT in the treatment of sleeping difficulties.

The sleep restriction method helps to promote a regular restful sleep pattern which becomes part of a person's daily routine. Many people who are depressed tend to spend too much time in bed (much of it not sleeping but rather worrying about it) or being plagued by intrusive thoughts. So, an association is made in the brain that the bed is a place of "worry and stress" rather than rest and restoration. It can also be a place of perceived "safety" in people who are severely depressed as they simply cannot get up to "face the world." In other words, they have lost hope, and although you may sleep when feeling like this, it is not of a good quality – neither restful nor restorative.

With the sleep restriction method, it is just that: restriction. If you reduce the amount of time physically spent in bed you are more likely to feel tired, and hence more likely to have restful, restorative sleep. You will not be spending hours upon hours, tossing, and turning in bed not being able to sleep. Often it is important, before starting to keep a sleep diary for a week before so you are fully aware of what your own sleeping patterns are (including the time spent in bed). You should go to bed feeling tired (rather than going to bed alert).

Once you are aware of your sleep patterns then basically you need to go to bed an hour later and set your alarm so you get up an hour earlier (even if you are tired you must get up). It is about establishing the sleep routine that will work best in the long run. Once you have established regular sleeping patterns and are going to bed when tired, then you can gradually increase the time in bed by going to bed earlier and getting up slightly later.

Briefly, bed should only be used for sleep or sex. Nothing else. Do not eat or drink in bed. Even light reading should be kept to a minimum and certainly no screen time (no phones or TV) in bed.

Sleep hygiene can also be incorporated into your bedtime routine. For example, make sure the room is neither too hot nor too cold. It should be very dark (we know that people have a more restful sleep when there are no extraneous light sources, such as a landing light or streetlights coming through curtains). Use blackout curtains or wear an eye mask. External noise can also affect the quality of sleep. This is especially so if you have a partner who snores loudly making it far more difficult to achieve a regular restful sleep. So, this is where wearing ear plugs can prove invaluable.

The point about a regular bedtime routine is to establish new habits that are achievable and will set fresh, positive ways in improving your mood. If you find yourself waking during the night (broken sleep is very common), get up and go to another room and do a light activity, such as reading or listening to a relaxation or guided meditation (no phones or TV though as these will only make you more alert, which will lead you to feeling stressed).

Whilst you are trying to establish a regular sleep routine it is important to keep a sleep and daily activity diary so that you can see what works best for you and to identify any triggers which lead to poor sleep patterns (so things like alcohol, coffee and drugs which act as stimulants). Also, you may like to identify any emotional and social triggers which impact on sleep quality. However, equally important in keeping a sleep and activity diary, is to notice when you have had a good night's sleep. In doing so, you will be more easily able to identify what led you to having a restful night. Aim, then to incorporate and replicate as many of the positive elements that worked for you into your nightly bedtime routine.

2) **As soon as you wake get up and make your bed and open the window.**

This provides a sense of closure on the night and the start of the new day). A made bed also prevents you wanting to get back in and lying in it all day! A made bed also feeds into a person's sense of achievement and mastery. Someone who is depressed or feels like all hope has gone, is more likely to not want to get out of bed in the first place. It is not uncommon for people who are low in mood to want to just stay in their beds all day. The making of the bed is also very important (in fact vital) to a sense of wellbeing. A made bed psychologically conveys a sense of order and calm. It also sends a message to the brain that you deserve a nice, fresh bed to get back into at the end of the day. An unmade bed sends the message of, "I have given up and it's not worth making my bed as I am just going to get back in – so why bother?" This is something I have heard time and time again in depressed patients, "why bother?" Well because you "matter" and you deserve it. You are worthy, that is why you "bother." You matter.

You should also open your bedroom window upon waking. This is essential (not merely to "air the room") but to establish closure on the night and the start of a new day. By opening the window, you allow the stale air of the night to escape and the fresh air of the coming day to enter. You connect yourself to the wider world outside and to nature (a core component of REMIND) by opening the window.

3) Shower or wash.

This should ideally be immediately upon waking. As soon as you wake up in the morning and have made the bed (or after, if you need the loo to empty your bladder), get up, go to the bathroom, and take a wash. Do not return to bed after your loo visit. Do not go down and make a hot drink before your morning wash. Why not you say? Well, getting up immediately upon waking and washing will significantly impact upon your mental wellbeing in a very positive way! There is emerging evidence that temperature changes in the body can have a direct impact upon mood and wellbeing. For example, a cold shower or warm bath have been shown to significantly improve mood and is sometimes an approach (temperature change) used in dialectical behaviour therapy (DBT). Even if you are going to do morning exercise, remember you can have another wash when you return from your workout! There are no rules saying you are only entitled to "one" wash a day.

If you have showered or washed, then it alters your frame of mind. It increases mental clarity and lessens the need to want to put your old night clothes/pyjamas back on and get back into bed! It also makes you more motivated to do your morning exercise.

When I was a newly qualified Occupational Therapist in the hospital (working on the care of the elderly wards) it was a common treatment approach to use washing and dressing practice first thing each morning. Not only did we look at the actual physical practice of washing but also its impact on task mastery, accomplishment, and self-care. Elderly patients are often physically frail and have a multitude of difficulties which can lead them to become dependent on others for their basic needs. However, maintaining one's independence for as long as possible links into a sense of control, routine and wellbeing.

Self-care links very closely to self-nurture. We know that people who become depressed or low in mood tend to ignore the vital aspects of putting the care they have shown to others into themselves (we will cover this concept in greater detail later when we discuss the "I" of the REMIND approach "Invest in self and others").

Regular washing and self-care lack the importance they once held if you have no routine or hope in life. I often hear the phrase, 'I just can't be bothered getting washed.' Having a wash as soon as you wake will really help how you feel about yourself and create a positive mindset that will set you up psychologically for the day ahead.

4) Dress for the day.

So now you have showered or washed for the day. Do you really want to put your old dirty nightclothes back on? In all honesty no. It does not make sense to put dirty clothes back onto a clean body. Nor does it make sense to put clean bedtime clothes back on to get back into a fully made-up bed! So, you are now in a position where you can put your daytime clothes on and begin the new start of a fresh day. A day filled with hope and optimism.

Following Your Routine

As a therapist, I know when people feel low in mood, that all the above four goals each morning, can feel like impossible and overwhelming tasks to achieve. However, try to stick with this basic routine as it really does help. Don't beat yourself up if you have days when you cannot achieve these. Keep going. Each day is a new start and a fresh opportunity to begin again. Even accomplishing just one or two of these can be "enough" when you are feeling overwhelmed with life.

Write down the above four step procedure and place it next your bed. You are far more likely to follow a set of goals if you see what the steps involved are in print. The brain is a curious thing indeed. Many people struggle with organisation and planning. You will know how difficult it is when you feel low, to even think straight and to complete the most basic of tasks. The smallest things, that many people take for granted, can seem like insurmountable mountains to climb. Basically, you simply do not know where to start and you quickly begin to feel overwhelmed by everything. However, what we do know, is that having things that you want to achieve written down make it far easier for your brain to see a clear pathway to succeed. This helps all people with planning and organisational difficulties (whether you suffer with low mood or not). So, get into the habit of writing things down, that way it will be easier to stick to your routine each morning. Also, once you have achieved your morning goals then you can see what you have accomplished, rather than what you have not. You will automatically send your brain the message that you are a success, which naturally raises both hope and optimism. So, write it down.

Another way of viewing the importance of a structured morning routine is rather like a foundation on which to base your day. So rather like underwear. It is the base layer on which to build upon and add complexity and interest. Remember, a routine reminds you of what you can control in your life (rather than what you cannot).

Affirmations and Gratitude

Affirmations are an extremely effective way of staying positive, being present in the moment whilst focusing on your goals and the day ahead. Affirmations should become part of your routine within the REMIND approach. In general, affirmations are normally stated in the present tense. For example, "I am" not "I was." They are always positive rather than negative statements. So, you would never say "I cannot" etc. They also need to be said with conviction avoiding things like: "I should" or "I might" etc. For them to work they need to be repeated so you build them into your routine.

Having a morning mantra/ affirmation can also set you up for a more optimistic and hopeful day ahead. It helps to have it written down so that you can read it aloud and it is visible when you awake.

The brain is programmed to favour negative thoughts. This is sometimes referred to as a "negative bias." This means that we pay more attention to negative intrusive thoughts, rather than positive and more realistic ones. Again, rather like the fight or flight response. It is thought that this negative bias is also a primitive way of being responsive to danger or threat. So, when our ancestors were living in the wild and were faced with an aggressor, the brain had to respond quickly to this negative threat. Therefore, this primitive survival instinct of a negative bias has continued. However, in many cases today, it serves little purpose but to reinforce negative and unhelpful ways of thinking. The good news is though, that we can re-train how we view things and can create more positive neural networks in our brains, rather than re-treading the old negative ones. Affirmations can really help you to establish a more optimistic and hopeful mindset.

One way of establishing a more positive mindset at the start of each day, is by expressing gratitude. Be thankful for all you have each day. Expressing thanks for what you have in life (rather than focusing on what is going wrong or what you do not have) helps to create a more positive and open mindset. It is the gratitude for the small everyday things that you have that provides the foundation for allowing greater wider change in other areas of your life.

When you first start to practice affirmations, it is quite common to feel a little uncomfortable about saying them. For example, it can feel like you are just "lying", and you don't believe it is true. This is normal. Many people feel this way at the start. However, it is quite important to do your best and to persevere. It gets easier as you begin to lay down positive networks in the brain. Your brain is programmed to favour negative thoughts, so it takes practice to form new positive ways of thinking.

Each section of the REMIND approach contains affirmations to help you to instil both positive ways of thinking, gratitude and the behaviour needed to make the changes necessary to lead a more fulfilled life.

Morning Routine Affirmations

Here are some examples of positive affirmations which you can write down and place directly next to your bed (or around your house where you can see them). It is important to place them in areas where you will see them easily and where you can read them aloud.

'I start this new day with hope.'

'I choose to be thankful for this new day.'

'Each day brings new possibilities for change.'

'I am open to learning new things.'

'I am excited for the new opportunities this day brings.'

'I am worthy of positive things this day.'

'I am grateful to feel alive.'

'I am grateful to the people in my life in this new day.'

'I am safe, calm and protected in this new day.'

'I choose a healthy way to be in this new day.'

'I am a unique person worthy of receiving good things.'

'I am thankful for all of the experiences to learn and grow today.'
'I accept myself this day.'

'I am enough this day.'

All the above are examples of positive affirmations. They also convey a sense of gratitude openness and acceptance too. You can choose any which you feel drawn to, or which resonate with you. Alternatively, why not design your own positive affirmation which touches on a personal level? Remember you have choice and control in life. You can choose to start each day and incorporate a positive way of thinking and being into your daily morning routine. It really will set you up well for the rest of the day.

Summary

Routine is a vital component for our mental and physical wellbeing. It provides a sense of safety, structure, and order within our lives. The four-step morning routine is a basic structure on which you can help to build a regular daily schedule which helps to set a positive and hopeful frame of mind on waking. The importance of both affirmations and expressing gratitude are a vital underpinning part of the REMIND approach. After this morning routine, there are several other key components which can then be incorporated into the rest of your day.

The REMIND approach includes the following ingredients within your routine: Exercise, mindfulness, invest in self and others and diet. All these concepts are vital to both getting fit and remaining mentally well. Therefore, each aspect of these should be incorporated into your daily routine. The trick is to consider what you can control, not what you cannot in an enjoyable and positive way.

The following chapters will cover each component of the REMIND approach in turn.

You can succeed and you are worthy of doing so. You can control your routine and reclaim your life.

Chapter 2
E = Exercise

'To Keep the body in good health is a duty, otherwise we shall not be able to keep our mind strong and clear.'
(Buddha)

Imagine feeling as you do now (or at your lowest ebb); you visit your doctor and he or she informs you about a new wonder drug which had just been invented. This new wonder drug would make you feel happier, increase energy, improve mental clarity, help you lose weight without dieting, give you a well-toned body, help you to sleep better, increase positivity, was free of charge and had no side effects…would you take it? The answer to this question is probably a resounding "yes, where can I get it from?" Well, the good news is, it has already been "invented." It is called "exercise." Yes, plain and simple exercise.

Exercise is vital to life. The human physical body is rather like a machine. If you do not use it then it ceases to work. However, you are far more than just your physical body of course. The mind, the body and the spirit are all inextricably linked. So therefore, purely from a basic level, exercise is an essential part of life and should therefore be built into your daily routine. It is essential.

Within some Western medical circles, the link between the mind-body and spirit have only just begun to be fully understood, in relation to their impact upon mood and motivation. Lorena Monda in her book, *The Practice of Wholeness: Spiritual Transformations in Everyday Life* (Monda, 2000) reports that the mind and body have never been seen as separate entities within Oriental Medicine. People are seen as "whole beings" with the mind, body and spiritual nature all given equal status and being inter-dependent. So, taking physical exercise is seen as an essential component of staying mentally and spiritually well. However, if you do not like the idea or the connotations of the word "spirit" then view this component as the "essence" of you. In other words, the qualities that make you a unique individual. You may have a physical body, a brain that works but these alone or together do not make you, you. There are clearly other aspects of the self. So, if you do not like the idea of "spirit" (you do not need to be religious or spiritual) think of the extra dimension alongside the mind and body as being your unique essence (or even your "higher self"). Whatever you feel comfortable with. Just have an open mind to the possibility of the added dimension to the qualities that make you a thinking and feeling person alongside your working brain and body.

As a therapist, one of the first things I ask my own clients is about how much physical exercise they build into their daily life. People normally come to see me at their lowest ebb, so unsurprisingly, physical exercise is either non-existent or extremely minimal. It becomes a vicious circle, you start to feel low, your energy drops, you develop generalised aches and pains, your sleep becomes disturbed (sleeping too much or very little) and the last thing you feel like doing is going for a "jog." People then become almost trapped in a downward spiral, where they begin to feel worse and worse about themselves. The negative physical feelings, feed into the negative thoughts.

What the Covid Pandemic did for many people, was to keep them "locked" into a situation where the increased barriers and opportunities to engaging in purposeful and meaningful physical activity were reduced to a virtual zero. Workouts at home became the only opportunities for many. However, for people, who were already experiencing low mood before the Pandemic broke, seeing so many exercising online, just served to reinforce a sense of failure in themselves. This was something I was hearing during my therapy sessions. However, beneficial physical exercise can be easy, simple, and accessible.

So, let's take a look at just why exercise is the "new wonder drug." Well, doctors are now prescribing structured exercise to many patients (Bergin, et al., 2020) because there is a growing body of scientific evidence which demonstrates that it can be as effective (if not more so) than taking medication. It can be used to treat patients with mild to moderate depression just as well as taking antidepressant medication but obviously without the resultant side effects.

A recent study in the USA, which was reported by Robinson and colleagues, by the Harvard School of Public health, found that the risks of developing a major depressive illness can be reduced by 26%, when people run for 15 minutes a day or walk for an hour. Exercise also helps people from relapsing back by creating a more positive frame of mind (Robinson et. al., 2021).

Gotschi and colleagues (2016) reported in their recent work, how back in 2008 the US Physical Activity Guidelines Committee published an extensive report summarising all the health benefits that exercise can have on a vast array of both mental and physical health conditions. This included improved cognitive function in elderly people (so not just in younger people).

On a physiological level, exercise stimulates all sorts of changes within the brain. It helps to support neural growth (forming more positive connections and pathways), it reduces inflammation, releases powerful endorphins and causes feel good mood stabilising serotonin to rise.

There is such an overwhelming body of evidence to support both the physical and mental health benefits of exercise, that it really can be classed as a "wonder drug." Due to all this data the World Health Organisation (WHO) in 2020 recommended that people should take a minimum of 150–300 minutes of moderate physical activity per week. So that is a minimum 21 minutes each day. Do you think that in a 24-hour period you could manage this to build it into your REMIND routine? In doing so you will be improving both your mental and physical wellbeing.

Physical exercise can also promote a feeling of calmness within the body too. One of my favourite senses within the body is something called proprioception. It is often overlooked within some of the scientific literature with the focus often being on the physiological changes occurring. However, proprioception is an essential sense in helping to calm a person and plays a vital role in exercise. Proprioception is the body's sense of knowing where it is in relation to its position in space, so you do not have to think consciously about the way you are moving. For example, if you are reading this now, you are probably sat or lying down, holding a book. Your brain knows this without consciously thinking about doing these things due to the proprioceptive feedback messages to your brain. Now, when a person has poor proprioception, they may appear to fidget a lot, they cannot keep still, they cannot calm down. They go into a spiral of sensory seeking. If you suffer from anxiety, you may recognise some of these symptoms in yourself. The sense they are seeking is by increasing proprioception from their muscles, tendons, and joints, so that the brain can help them to make sense of the here and now.

Proprioception helps to calm a person down. Have you ever looked at new-born babies in hospitals and how they are "wrapped" in sheets or blankets? Midwives often "swaddle" the baby by crossing a folded sheet across their shoulders so that the baby's arms are held close into the body. This helps to calm the baby down and make them feel safe by providing deep pressure (or proprioception) from fixed points on the body. It is also one of the reasons why weighted blankets and tucking sheets in, around people work so well in promoting a more restful sleep too.

When I was involved in developing the Global children's television series, *Tree Fu Tom*, one of the reasons we built exercises that facilitated proprioception into many of the movement spells, was to help the children to gain a greater sense of body awareness and how they were feeling the movements in relation to their position in space. This is something that many children with certain conditions like dyspraxia and ADHD struggle with. So, it plays a valuable part in both learning and acquiring new skills, whilst also improving how you feel when you move your body.

Now, when we exercise proprioception really comes into value. You get constant messages from the body to tell the brain about how and where it is moving. The best exercises for increasing proprioception are repetitive (so from fixed points) which also provide deep pressure (from the muscles, tendons, and joints). It is also one of the reasons why progressive muscle relaxation is so effective in promoting a sense of calm.

So, in other words, exercise is an essential tool to both improve mood and increase energy. Yet it can also be a vital component to calm you down and make you relaxed. Exercise is both vitalising and soothing. What a "drug" hey?

Excuses, Excuses

But if you are reading this, you probably know that exercise is good for you already? But what you probably do not know is how to break the cycle of inertia, so that you can start moving and begin. It is the initial start that almost everyone (whether you suffer from low mood or not) finds difficult. Procrastination is the greatest hurdle to overcome in the battle of mood versus exercise.

Self-imposed barriers are often your worst enemy. I think I have heard most of the "excuses" (sorry, "reasons") why a person cannot do exercise. For example, common reasons include: "not having the time", "not having the money", "not having the ability", "not having the space", "having health concerns" etc., etc. The list of reasons is endless. But so are the possibilities too.

However, exercise should be based on ability. So, in other words, what you can do rather than what you cannot (at present at least). I have worked a lot over the years with people with some extremely severe physical disabilities. There is almost always a form of exercise which a person can do, regardless of physical impairment. It is about looking at where both your skills and enjoyment lie. By taking a "can do" rather than a "can't do" attitude, the possibilities are endless. For example, like most people I have enjoyed watching the Olympic Games on television. For me the Para Olympics, is the most inspirational part. Observing athletes who have overcome impairments and barriers in life to reach the optimum level of peak human achievement, is indeed humbling and inspiring. Exercise is achievable for all regardless of disability. So, always look at where your skills lie and what ability you have when you approach exercise.

The key to successful exercise is:

1) **Achievable.**
2) **Enjoyable.**
3) **Sustainable.**

Where Do I Start?

'Any movement no matter how big or small is better than none.'

The above mantra is one I use all the time. The point is, not to put any pressure upon yourself when starting exercise. Procrastination is normally the biggest hurdle and a sense of feeling guilty if you are totally unmotivated or low in mood. Be gentle on yourself when building it into your daily routine. The whole point of exercise is that no matter how much or little you do, any is better than none. If you set goals that are neither achievable nor sustainable, you are not going to enjoy the process or stay motivated. So, if you create a more positive mindset of "any exercise is better than none", it will make your goal of building exercise into your daily routine far more doable from the start. Remember too, that exercise is simply a form of "play."

The following affirmations will help create a more positive frame of mind, say them out loud each day:

'I enjoy physical movement.'
'Any movement is better than none at all.'
'I am thankful for the ability to enjoy exercise.'

Enjoyable

Find an exercise that is fun to do that you will enjoy. For many of my clients, there have been negative associations with "exercise" going way back to school and structured

Physical Exercise (PE) lessons. Mentally, the connections between bad experiences and physical exercise have been set from a young age. This means that the brain links distress to the word "exercise." So as a therapist, I fully understand the reluctance of some to build exercise into their daily lives. However, formal exercise is only one tiny part of human movement and physical activity. There are a multitude of different ways to engage with enjoyable physical exercise that are easy and fun to do.

Small Steps – 30 Second Rule

So, you have entered a positive way of approaching exercise. What next? Well, some psychologists and therapists use a technique called the "five minute rule", whereby you set yourself the small goal of exercising for just five minutes. At the end of the five minutes, you can either stop or carry on if you feel like it. That way you have set a goal that is achievable. This is a nice, simple way of overcoming the first hurdle of procrastination.

However, for some people, even the five minute rule can feel like an insurmountable hurdle. So, in this case reduce it. Give yourself 30 seconds! I call this the "30 second rule." Remember your positive mantra of "any movement is better than none at all." The trick is to move and to start now. If you start with the aim of 30 seconds you will find that you are likely to continue beyond this. However, 30 seconds is more psychologically achievable than five minutes when you are feeling at your lowest. So be gentle on yourself.

One really good way of achieving this is to start with an intense form of exercise to get the heart rate pumping and to immediately raise the mood. My personal 30 second favourite is to get up and to do "on the spot marching." Make sure you raise your knees as you do so, and stomp down with your feet as hard as you can, whilst swinging both arms in a "marching motion." Sometimes it helps to do this marching exercise on a hard, or wooden, floor, so that you get the audible feedback. The sound of you "marching" also helps to act as a mindful cue which helps keep your attention focused on the exercise. The key really is to get up and start moving.

Dance, Dance, Dance.

Dance is an integral part of human nature. Humans have always danced. There is evidence that our earliest ancestors used dance as part of religious and shamanic ceremonies. Dance is one of the most accessible ways to instantly start exercising. The key is to have the right music that you like which triggers the desire to get up and start.

Many years ago, I was working at a nursing home for elderly people who had mental health difficulties. The challenge for me was to find a form of physical activity which could be enjoyed by all, and which would be of benefit both mentally and physically. I introduced dance, by playing the music that the residents liked. The key was the music. The music was the tool which enabled the dance to take place. The tunes that were played all held personal meaning to the residents. Before I started, I asked the residents, what sort of music they enjoyed? I was a young 21-year-old at the time, trying to find suitable music for people who were 50 years plus older than myself. So, it was important to discover the right music. I found that most of the residents in the nursing home wanted to hear music which took them back to their youth, and to times when life seemed "better." Strangely, all the songs chosen were from around Word War Two, as it reminded them of their youth. So, in other words the music held personal meaning for them. What I noticed, was that even the most physically disabled resident could join in even if they were able to just move their hands to sway in time with the music. The mood of the residents also increased significantly during and after the dance sessions. So, no matter how much or little the residents were able to move, the sessions always improved how they felt.

So, if you are reading this, why not try it? Make a list of your favourite songs. Play them, get up and start dancing. See how you feel. You can easily build dance into your everyday routine. It is that simple. It will improve your mood straight away by increasing serotonin and raising your heart rate. You do not need any expensive equipment. Play your favourite music each day. Set this as one of your SMART goals and build it into your routine.

Dance Affirmations.
'Dance makes me feel good.'
'I love to dance to my favourite tunes.'
'Exercise is easy with dance.'
'I am grateful for having music I love that I can dance to.'

Housework as Exercise

Another achievable way to increase physical activity is by doing simple daily chores, such as cleaning, washing, vacuuming etc. Housework is both purposeful and meaningful physical activity. The key is to make the chores achievable. So, in the previous chapter I discussed the importance of a daily morning routine and the making of the bed upon waking. Well, one of the things that helps with psychological wellbeing is being in an environment which is clean and clutter free.

Therefore, housework holds both a purpose and a meaning in engaging in more physical exercise, which has an end goal which directly impacts upon your mood.

During lockdown, like many therapists, my work with patients and clients was online via Zoom. What this did, was to allow me access to people's homes in a way I had never had before. I was able to gain important snap shots of their personal spaces during some of the lowest points in their lives. I could always tell when things were starting to spiral out of control by the amount of washing in the background, whether they were seeing me in bed or with an unmade bed behind themselves, etc. The fact is, having a tidy environment really does have a positive impact on our mental wellbeing and a good way to build some achievable physical exercise into your daily routine is via everyday housework. Like dance, play your favourite music (the louder the better to help release those endorphins) whilst you are doing your chores.

Housework Affirmations.
'A clean and tidy home makes me feel good.'
'I enjoy living in a tidy home.'
'I enjoy doing the housework.'
'I am grateful of having a home which I enjoy cleaning.'

Walking

Walking is such an important exercise. It holds both purpose and meaning too, as walking is a form of transporting you to places without relying on transport. If you are fortunate to have the ability to walk, then do it. It requires no expensive gym equipment or special clothing. Whether you live in a city or in the rural countryside you can walk.

The trick with walking is not to procrastinate. Get up and get out. Walk for as long or as little as you want but just get out and do it.

Social anxiety is often a major barrier in preventing people from walking outside. If this is the case then choose a time of day when there is likely to be less people about (such as very early in the morning) and start by going for short, manageable walks. Build this up as you gain confidence both psychologically and physically. You can plan your route ahead, so you know what to reasonably expect. Once you feel more confident try experimenting with different times of the day so you can build up resilience and distress tolerance (both vital in good mental health).

Walking in nature is one of the most beneficial ways of boosting mental wellbeing and we will cover the vital role of nature in a later chapter, when we more completely discuss the "N" in the REMIND approach. If you can walk in nature, such as a park, a tree lined street or a field then even better, you will be boosting your wellbeing even further.

If you have ever visited a public gymnasium or sports centre, you will notice that there are treadmills in there. Now treadmills are normally associated with running yet, it is amazing how many people use them for gentle walking. There are number of reasons for this. Firstly, walking is a valuable form of exercise. Secondly, people often join gyms because they want to get fit, so they will start at the level they feel comfortable with, and can achieve. Thirdly, there is a sense of community and "belonging" when joining a gym, which makes building exercising into a regular routine more sustainable too. Fourthly, (and most importantly), they enjoy walking.

Lots of people now use step counters which measure how many steps people have used during the day. However, although these are really good tools to measure both achievement and progress, some people find they can actually act as barriers to exercise. For example, someone told me about how they were given a step counter as a present. This person was feeling quite "down" at the time and the last thing she felt like doing was wearing her step counter just to be told she was not being "active enough." She felt as though it just reinforced the fact that she was a failure by telling her she was not exercising enough. So, although some people find these gadgets good tools for motivation, some do not. It is about removing barriers and obstacles to participation and enjoying exercise, so it becomes an automatic thing that you just do without having to think too deeply about it.

Another good trick to do when walking is to wear a back-pack over BOTH shoulders. Why? Well, remember I mentioned about one of my favourite senses being proprioception earlier? Wearing a backpack helps to calm you as it facilitates proprioception by placing constant deep pressure across your shoulder muscles by stretching them. It helps to relax the muscles. If you have ever suffered from stress and anxiety, you will notice that you often feel tension or pain between your shoulder blades and in your neck. One of the reasons for this is because the large muscles here naturally start to tense in response to stress, back to the old primitive "fight or flight response", where you may need to stay and face your aggressor or run away. However, by wearing a back-pack on your walk, not only will you be able to carry useful items, but you will also actually feel much more relaxed and less stressed whilst doing so. And the positive thing is, you will enjoy your daily walk much more if you feel calmer.

Walking Affirmations
'Walking keeps me fit.'
'I can walk, and I enjoy walking.'
'My walking helps me to relax.'
'I am thankful for the ability to walk.'
'I feel good when I walk.'

Cycling

Cycling is my ultimate all-time favourite form of exercise for mind body and spirit. I am slightly biased as I have been a life-long cyclist since the age of 13, when I joined my first cycling club, and I started racing. I am also married to a former professional racing cyclist and ex-British Champion. Although I no longer race, I make the time to ride my bike most days (even if it is just to my local village shop). I am grateful that I found an exercise at such a young age which has endured throughout my life. It is more than just a mere form of physical exercise. It is part of me. Cycling is part of my identity, my being. It feeds into my mind, body, and spirit (or my unique essence that makes me who I am).

In the UK, there is a national problem with obesity. So, in 2020 the Government started to encourage doctors to prescribe cycling to tackle this problem. However, cycling being prescribed for health, rather than medication is not a new phenomenon. For example, in Belgium (which is often referred to as the "home of cycling") doctors routinely prescribe cycling for a whole range of physical and mental health difficulties, both alongside and instead of medication.

Cycling Affirmations
'I love riding my bike.'
'Each ride on my bike brings new adventures.'
'I feel joy on my bike in all weathers and seasons.'
'I love to feel the wind in my hair/ face/ skin as I cycle.'
'I use my bike to travel to help the environment.'

Running

Running or jogging is the next level up from walking. You will obviously need to be able to access suitable running shoes and sports clothes. However, the benefits of regular running cannot be understated in terms of both cardiovascular health and mental health.

Running can be completed (like walking) as both a solitary activity and a social one too. It can also be competitive. If you enjoy running, then do it. Start off small and do not overdo it. Always warm up and cool down with simple stretches so you minimize any risks of injury (another barrier).

Running Affirmations
'I feel exhilarated running.'
'Running helps me to focus.'
'I feel relaxed when I run.'
'I love to run.'
'I am grateful for the gift of running.'

Time of Day

One of the things I get asked a lot about is, "When is the best time to exercise?" Well, there are no hard and fast rules here. However, most therapists advise clients to structure it so they can do it first thing in the morning. There are several reasons for this (including some physiological benefits), however, my favourite reason is that it puts you into a more positive mindset for the day ahead. If you begin the day with exercise (following your set morning routine) you are more likely to incorporate it into a regular schedule. Starting your day with exercise can improve mental clarity and provide a sense of optimism.

The earlier you get up and start seems to have some benefits too. I often go out cycling at 6 am in the morning (before there is a lot of traffic about). I call it, "When the world is waking up." It is a very special time of the day, and you will notice, sights, sounds and smells that you are not normally aware of at other times of the day too. For example, the dew on the grass, the morning mist, cobwebs on trees with droplets of water on them that sparkle like jewels. You will get to notice the same people, out walking, exercising their dogs, running, commuting, and cycling too. People also seem to be more receptive to saying "hello" at this time too. It is almost as though you are part of a special "club." There is a sense of belonging. I find that early morning exercise is a good way of blending the mind, body, and spiritual side of our natures.

However, if you cannot face the prospect of early morning exercise, remember that any exercise is good, regardless of the time of day. I have one client who finds that running at night-time helps him to de-stress after a hard day at work. He prefers to run when it is dark as there is less traffic on the roads, and it helps him to focus. He tells me, that he notices (and sees) lots of nocturnal nature activity during his nightly runs, such as bats, foxes, badgers, and owls. Animals you do not normally see during the daylight. He has scheduled nightly running into his daily routine so that even if he has faced an extremely stressful day, he always has the hope and optimism of his nightly run.

You can also break your daily exercise down into smaller, achievable blocks throughout the day, rather than doing it all in one go. Find a way of fitting the "E" of the REMIND approach into your daily routine so you will start to feel more positive and in control. The possibilities are endless with exercise.

Case Study

Brian

Brian came to see me as a "last resort" due to long standing complex trauma resulting from witnessing atrocities during his active military service. He had been signed off from work due to his ongoing battle with depression and was now the "stay at home father" looking after his two children, whilst his partner went to work. This had fed into his sense of failure as a father and a "provider."

When Brian came to see me, he was extremely inactive. He had gained a lot of weight due to comfort eating and inactivity, his GP was primarily concerned that he was going to develop obesity related problems, such as Type two diabetes. However, Brian's low mood and reluctance to exercise was a major hurdle.

One week we had a breakthrough, and it was due to cycling. His young son had been given a new bicycle for his birthday from his grandparents. He wanted to ride to the local play park (which was a short distance from their home) but Brian could not keep up with walking alongside him, due to his weight. His goal was that he wanted to be able to keep up with his son.

However, as his child was getting better and quicker at riding his bike, Brian quickly realised that he needed to find another way. And you guessed it, Brian bought himself a bike so that he could cycle alongside his young child to the park so he could keep up with him. Then he started to enjoy their daily cycling trips more and more. He started to lose weight, he began to feel better about himself, he binged less on food and his fitness increased. Slowly but surely, Brian's mental and physical wellbeing improved. He started to cycle when his children were at school during the day, going further and further distances. He enjoyed cycling so much that it has now become part of his daily routine. Cycling literally saved him.

Summary

Exercise is a deeply unique and individual experience. The trick is to find a way that works for you, so that it is enjoyable, sustainable and can be built into your daily routine. Move more and you will start to feel better both physically and mentally. Start with small achievable steps and build up gradually. You will, and can, get there!

Chapter 3
M = Mindfulness

'Depression is a condition of the past, whilst anxiety is a condition of the future.'

The above saying is frequently said in therapy about anxiety and depression. Our thoughts keep us prisoners to our feelings, and this then results in behaviours which lead to these "conditions." Obviously, there is a lot more to it in terms of both anxiety and depression in terms of causes. However, in simple terms, if we can live more fully in the present moment it can go a long way in terms of helping mental wellbeing and in our own personal enjoyment and participation in life. Stress, in all its various disguises is an inevitable part of life. This is a fact. No one who has ever lived (or will live in the future) can escape the stress of life. Life is not a steady ride. This is where mindfulness can help in terms of keeping us connected to the present instead of living our lives in an anxious future state, or a depressed past one.

What Is Mindfulness?

'Yesterday is history, tomorrow is a mystery, today is a gift – that is why we call it the present.'
(Author unknown)

Mindfulness in its most basic form is being fully present in whatever you are doing or experiencing with an open mind, non-judgmentally and with interest. It is simply focused attention in the moment. It is not about being fully "self-absorbed" in your thoughts though. Not at all. Mindfulness allows us to experience life and to capture a full awareness of what is happening whilst it is happening. At the same time, mindfulness prevents us from being absorbed in our random, automatic, wandering thoughts. It is these intrusive thoughts which often prevent us from living fully in the present moment and enjoying all that life has to offer. It keeps us both connected to the world around us and lets us feel our place within that world too. So, in other words, we have a greater interest and feel more in tune with ourselves and in those around us too.

Mindfulness has been found to be so effective in helping people to reclaim control over their thoughts and subsequent behaviour, that many "third wave" cognitive therapies now include it as part of their treatment protocol. These include mindfulness-based cognitive therapy (MBCT), mindfulness-based stress reduction (MBSR), acceptance and commitment therapy (ACT) and dialectical behavioural therapy (DBT).

However, mindfulness is by no means a "new" concept which has been adopted and adapted by psychological therapists (myself included). Christopher Titmuss in his book, *Mindfulness for Everyday Living* (Titmuss, 2014) explains how it has been at the heart of Buddhist tradition for over 2,500 years. Titmuss, himself is a former Buddhist monk in Thailand, who spent six years there before returning to the West and using these teachings and practices as a guiding force for his new life.

Titmuss believes that mindfulness can be used to enhance all areas of your life to open your awareness to a new appreciation of life and your place in this world. He believes that it can change our relationship with everything around us so that we can become more in tune with who we really are, with other people and with what is happening around us.

Mindfulness works because it teaches us to focus all our attention into whatever task we are engaging with in a non-judgmental way but also with interest. These things can be as simple as cleaning the surfaces of the kitchen, opening the mail, picking weeds from your garden, walking to the shops, etc. This list is endless. The main point is that you fully immerse yourself in the task in hand and give it your full attention, so that you too can be fully present in every moment that you are alive.

Firstly, it is important to see how "un-mindful" we have become to fully appreciate what mindfulness really is and how we can all benefit from learning this useful skill. For example, multitasking, texting, whilst watching the television, whilst chatting to the person next to you, at the same time as sipping your cup of tea. Or maybe, you drive to work whilst daydreaming then arrive at your destination without even knowing how you have arrived there. Or perhaps, you have sat watching a film on the television and before you know it that whole packet of biscuits, bottle of wine, bag of chips etc. has just "disappeared" and you have no idea whatsoever, where they went. Maybe, you are working right now at your computer, whilst eating lunch but you have no idea where that sandwich went? Perhaps you are on social media, and you quickly respond to any posts or messages? Does this sound familiar? Unfortunately, many people have lost the ability to be mindful, so that they are spending their lives existing like this. They are never present in the moment, and they do not engage fully in just one thing.

Mindfulness in a World Obsessed with Social Media

Social media can be both a blessing and a curse. Although you may think you are focusing your attention fully on the present whilst attending to your screen, you are not. I often think that social media use is one of the reasons why as a species we have become less connected to living our own lives in the best way possible. I have noticed how over the years many students seem less connected to their studies and more connected to gaining "instant" knowledge at the flick of a switch rather than the whole process of learning and consolidation.

During the Pandemic the use of social media did have several positive aspects. In fact, those positive qualities of creating a sense of community and feeling connected to others to break down isolation, were (and continue to be) invaluable.

However, one of the overwhelming negative aspects is overusing social media so that it becomes an addiction. How often have you sat in a café or restaurant and witnessed people out for a meal sat engrossed on their phones, rather than engaging with the people they are out with? This is something I see all the time and it has become quite normalised within Western culture. But it is a prime example of not being present; in other words, not being mindful.

Overusing social media can lead you to feeling dissatisfied with your own life if you are constantly being bombarded with images and stories of others looking amazing, doing wonderful things, and having expensive holidays/ cars etc. Remember, that people post only the things they want you to see. Often, even celebrities are not fully engaging in their own lives and are often not that happy with life themselves. So social media can create a false image of aspiration. Therefore, reducing the time you spend on social media or using it in a more focused way so that you engage only with close friends or family can significantly help your mental wellbeing and make you more mindful.

How to Do Social Media Mindfully:

1) **Have a digital detox, by completely coming off all social media and putting your attention into something you have always wanted to do. For example, a hobby, a new skill or reading a book.**

2) **If you cannot face coming off social media, then reduce your time on it.**

3) **Build in a set time each day when you will check your social media (this includes work related emails too!). Stick to this time and do not deviate from it. You can build this into your REMIND routine. I normally recommend no more than one hour each day at a maximum (less than this is better).**

4) **Use this set time to fully focus your attention on responding to messages etc. Do not do two things (or multiple tasks) at the same time.**

5) **Put your device into a drawer so that you are not tempted to check.**

6) **When going to bars, restaurants, cafes etc. Do not check your phone. Give the person you are with your full attention – not your phone. Keep your phone firmly in your pocket or bag.**

7) **Be present in the moment fully and do not spend your time living in the future or past by scrolling through endless irrelevant social media posts.**

Ocean Mind Mindfulness

The metaphor of the mind being like the ocean is an excellent way of viewing how mindfulness works. It was first coined by Jon Kabat-Zinn in his book, *Wherever You Go, There You Are* (Kabat-Zinn, 2019). He suggests that for you to see how mindfulness works it can be helpful to view the mind as being like the surface of a lake or an ocean. It changes from being rough to smooth and tranquil; but it is always in a state of change.

Similarly, in Dialectical Behaviour Therapy, (DBT) using the metaphor of "waves" is frequently used with patients to help them better understand how to regulate their moods, feelings and emotions. Learning to metaphorically "surf" is good way of understanding how the many "waves" of life and stresses will come and go and how nothing is permanent. Using mindfulness as a way of "surfing" them will enable you to cope much better without "sinking" beneath the waves of life. So, if you view your troubles like waves which vary in sizes, shapes, intensities, influenced by external sources you can see that mindfulness can be a way of dealing with changing moods and emotions. The ocean will always be there (just as your mind will always be there) but the waves and storms will only ever be temporary – just like your troubles. This interesting concept is a really helpful way in building your distress tolerance and resilience during the tough times of life.

Thoughts as Clouds Mindfulness

A big part (or barrier) to living fully in the present moment are our thoughts. Or rather those annoying intrusive thoughts. The self-doubt, the negative mindless chatter, that can seem relentless and prevents us from enjoying and being present fully in the moment.

A good metaphor to use here is to view yourself as the "sky" and your thoughts as being "clouds" that constantly pass over the sky. Observe these clouds but do not pass judgement on them. Allow the thoughts to come and view them as being clouds passing across a clear sky. Sometimes these clouds may seem dense, with only small glimpses of the sky. Other times, the clouds are light and fluffy and pass easily across a clear sky. But always know, that just like your thoughts, the clouds will pass. The clouds (like your thoughts) are not permanent – they are ever changing. Observe them but do not pass any judgement. Let them pass and stay focused in all you do in the present moment. Remember you are the sky and that is constant. The clouds will pass, and they never stay.

Become Childlike

Adults have much to learn from children – rather than the other way around. In fact, becoming more childlike and approaching everyday tasks with a childlike curiosity can really help us in our quest to building mindfulness into our everyday lives.

The next time you are around a child, spend time to observe how they fully and completely seem to absorb themselves into their everyday occupations, especially play. This includes both solitary play and shared occupations. They are fully able to immerse themselves into the activity so that they are experiencing every aspect of it. If you look at children in other situations, you will see that they give whatever they do their full attention (even children with attentional difficulties will immerse themselves far better within activities than many adults). Children do not seem to have the perception of time that adults do as they are far more focused on the present and do not tend to be thinking ahead or to past events whilst they are engaging in activities.

Practical Mindful Activities

In terms of the REMIND approach it is important to build mindfulness into your everyday life, so that it becomes an instinct. A good way of starting is through our five senses. The purpose of the following activity commonly used in DBT is to experience the world more mindfully through your five senses: Touch, sight, smell, sound, and taste.

Mindful Touch

1) **Whilst walking pay attention to how your feet feel with each step: Your heel pressing against the floor; the sensation in the arch of your foot; your toes. Try walking barefoot on different surfaces (ie. carpet, tiles, grass, sand etc).**

2) **Relax into a bed, chair, or sofa. Pay attention to how your body feels as it relaxes back. Pay attention to how your body feels supported and the pressure of it against your body. Work downwards from your head, neck, shoulders, arms, hands, back, chest, tummy, hips, thighs, knees, lower legs, and feet, scanning your body.**

3) Whilst bathing, pay attention to how the water, soap, shower gel, flannels etc. feel against your skin and how they smell. Notice the temperature of the water and how it makes you feel. Whilst drying your body, be mindful of how the towel feels and the sensation it produces against your skin as you dry your body.

Mindful Sight

1) Stand in front of an object, picture, or view from a window that you walk past each day. Look at every single detail as though you are viewing it for the first time.

2) Stand in front of the mirror and practice moving your face in lots of different poses. Pay attention to all the different parts and shapes of your face as it moves.

3) Go outside and gaze upwards to the sky. Watch as the clouds move and constantly change shape in the sky. Observe fully the structure and formation of the clouds and the sensations of the weather against your face and skin as you gaze upwards (you can also do this at night looking at the stars).

Mindful Smell

1) Whilst putting the laundry away, pull out a freshly washed item and inhale the scent.

2) If you have a favourite perfume spray some into the air. Experience the smell as though it is the first time you are sensing it. Pay attention to the different parts of the scent and what you notice about it.

3) Whilst outside pay attention to the different smells. As you walk the scents in the air will change as you experience different scenery. Experience seasonal smells (summer, autumn, winter, and spring). Pay attention to the smells associated with the time of day, morning, lunch time and evening.

Mindful Sound

1) Sit outside alone and just listen to the noises around you. Pay careful attention to the noises you can hear, traffic, bird song, people talking, the wind blowing, dogs barking etc. What sorts of noises can you hear? Can you notice the sounds of nature around you?

2) Listen carefully to strangers speaking. Pay attention to the tone and the pitch of their voice. Do they have an accent? Pay attention to the speed at which they speak, the pauses they make and

when they take a breath. What are they truly saying?

3) Play your favourite piece of music and listen carefully to it as though it is the first time you have heard it. What do you notice? What do you enjoy?

Mindful Taste

1) Prepare your favourite food. Sit at a table and switch off any phones or distractions. Mindfully and slowly savour each mouthful as though you are eating it for the first time. Focus all your attention to the taste, temperature, and sensation of the food as you slowly devour each mouthful.

2) Place a sweet or savoury item in your mouth and pay careful attention to the taste and texture as it dissolves on your tongue.

3) Try the "raisin experiment." This is often used in CBT to teach people how mindfulness works. Take a raisin and slowly begin to chew. Do not swallow but focus all your attention to how the raisin feels within your mouth, taste, texture, and sensations. Pay attention to how your mouth feels as it sucks and chews the raisin. Give the raisin and the process of slowly savouring it your full concentration. You may even close your eyes to focus. In doing so you are becoming mindful.

Mindful Affirmations
'I live in the present moment.'
'I am fully open to experiencing all that I do.'
'I am grateful for this moment to experience all that it has to offer.'
'I exist in the present, not in the past or the future.'
'All joy of life is available in this present moment.'

Mindful De-Clutter

'Have nothing in your house that is not useful or
beautiful; if such a rule were followed out, you would be
astonished at the amount of rubbish you would get
rid of.'
(Oscar Wilde)

Take a good look around your home and see how true the above quotation by the famous author Oscar Wilde really is. Although it was written over 100 years ago at a time when as a society, we were less consumerist, it is even more relevant now than when it was originally penned. The fact is we live with far too many "things" than we either need or want.

Physical clutter around you can cause the mind to become overwhelmed and saturated. Researchers, Stephanie McMains and Sabine Kastner published a study in 2011 which found that clutter and being disorganised can have a negative cumulative effect on the brain, which can lead to feelings of being "drained" and a loss of ability to focus. Just having the visual distraction of clutter around you causes the brain to feel overloaded which can then negatively impact on your working memory (McMains and Kastner, 2011).

We work far better when there is order and calm and that includes our physical surroundings. This is backed by the research of McMains and Kastner (2011), who propose that just clearing the clutter at home and work can have a positive impact on your ability to process information and focus your attention on the task in hand. In turn, this can then lead to increased productivity.

An untidy home can make you feel anxious and even depressed as can having too many physical objects around you. They act as a source of stimulation. For example, just notice how you feel when you enter natural, and uncluttered environments – calmer. Pay mindful and careful attention to the sorts of environments that make your mood better or worse. You will soon notice and recognise a pattern that starts to emerge. Researchers have found a link between the stress hormone cortisol and living in a cluttered home. One study found that women who reported higher levels of stress also had increased depressed mood over the course of the day who lived in cluttered homes. This was compared with women who reported lower levels of stress and depressed mood who lived in homes that were restorative and calming (Saxbe and Repetti, 2009).

An interesting study in 2015 by Amanda Raines and her colleagues found that people who live in extremely cluttered homes were at far greater risk of obesity and binge eating than those who live in tidy uncluttered environments (Raines et al, 2015). So not only can clutter impact upon how you feel but it can also translate to comfort eating and binge eating as your life begins to spiral out of control.

It is vital to apply mindfulness to your home and to create the sort of living space that will both soothe the soul yet feed the mind in a positive and productive way. That starts with mindful de-cluttering the possessions that are neither "beautiful nor useful." In short, all the "stuff" around you that is holding you back in life.

Clothing

If you do not know where to start, then begin with your clothes. This is always the easiest place and the area where accumulation begins. Most people have clothes they have never worn in their wardrobe and even more astonishing, do not fit them. Women particularly are guilty of this. Many women live their lives living in the future by holding onto clothes that are far too small for them, for the time they manage to lose weight. In doing so, they are not living their lives in the present. In other words, not leading a mindful life. Never hold onto clothes that do not fit "just in case." If they are too small now (and you are not working towards an imminent weight loss goal), then get rid of them. All they are serving to do is either remind you of your younger days (when you were slimmer) by keeping you locked into the past or reinforcing your sense of present dissatisfaction with how you look right now and the longing for the future. If you do eventually lose that weight, ask yourself this question – will this item of clothing still be worth wearing or even "fashionable?"

Now look at all the clothes that fit you right now. Which ones do you wear daily? Keep these. Which ones have you not worn in over a year? Lose these. Which clothes do I love that I only wear on special occasions? Wear these now! It is the clothes we keep for "best" that have the potential to improve our mental wellbeing right now. This links to investing in ourselves and self-care. Never save clothes for the future. Are there clothes in your wardrobe that you did not even know existed, but you love? Well, wear them. Any clothes that do not fill you with joy when you look at them, or those that make you feel great when you wear them, well they can go.

Be mindful and immerse yourself in this process. Pay very careful attention to the feelings associated with clothes. If they make you feel good wearing them right now keep them. If they are too small or big never keep them "just in case" your shape changes. Live your life for now. If you do eventually lose all the weight, well you can then engage in mindful shopping for a new wardrobe.

As you go through your wardrobe have empty bags ready to discard unwanted clothes. Donate to charity where possible as this will feed into a sense of wellbeing by investing in others. Recycle any particularly worn or damaged clothes (never hold onto these). If you have clothes that are in a new condition, then take photos and upload them immediately to sell online if necessary. The trick is to get rid of these bags as quickly as possible so that they do not find their way back into your wardrobe.

Immerse yourself mindfully into your wardrobe de-clutter and notice how liberating it feels when you see a clearer rack of wearable clothes emerging. Keep focused on the present and avoid the temptation to indulge in memories of the last time you wore that dress ten years ago. It is about the present not the past or future. Do not let sentimentality creep in.

I once did this process with my own wardrobe, and I ended up with 13 bags of clothes which I sent off to the local charity shops. I felt liberated! I ended up with a coordinated row of clothes that I really enjoy wearing right now and which make me feel good.

Clothes can either keep us locked into living a life in the future or past, but they also have the power of allowing us to live a more mindful life in the present.

De-Clutter Those Cupboards

When your cupboards are full, then you have nowhere to store things, leading to what I call, "chaos on the surfaces." It does not matter how big or small your home is, if you have cupboards, then you will fill them with things you do not really need or want.

One of the biggest offenders is the kitchen cupboard. It is amazing how many out-of-date foodstuffs you will find in there. If the food is out of date get rid of it. Why is it still in there?

The crockery cupboards can be filled with odd cups, broken plates, pans with missing handles etc. Look mindfully at these items. Ask yourself this question, "Do I use these on a daily basis?" If not, these can go. Are there items which you only save for best? If so, start using them now, never save for "best", live in the present not the future. Treat yourself with care. If you are eating your meals from a broken plate but you have beautiful crockery in your cupboard, what sort of message are you truly sending to yourself? You are saying that you are not worthy of good things!

Take a look at the amount of beautiful dinner sets that can be routinely found in charity shops or from house clearances after the previous owner has passed away. These can often appear to be in pristine condition – even though they may be several decades old. That person was saving their things for "best" and that time seldomly came and now they are dead, and their treasured "things" are being offered at bargain prices. The owner of that fine porcelain was not living mindfully in the present and clearly did not get to use their "lovely" things on a daily basis. This can be a truly humbling lesson. Use your favourite and most treasured items daily. You are worthy of the best.

Be ruthless in your de-cluttering and get rid of anything that does not fill you with joy.

Keep all surfaces in your kitchen clear. Do not use worktops or tables to store items that do not fit into your cupboards. As humans, we do not need anywhere near the number of things that we think we do. So, try to live a more simplistic and uncluttered life. Wash and keep clear all surfaces as this will help you to feel more in control and less overwhelmed.

Living Room De-Clutter

Look at your living room. Next to your bedroom this is the place where people spend most of their time. Therefore, it is also the place that needs careful attention and focus in terms of both decluttering and cleaning. A clean and tidy room will raise your spirits and have an enormous impact on mood and how you enjoy using this space. You will feel calmer and more content in the present moment, in a room that is clean and clutter free.

Get rid of any excessive ornaments or objects. Apply the wise words of Oscar Wilde in terms of only having beautiful (and minimal) objects in your living space.

Photograph De-Clutter

De-clutter photographs. I do not mean by throwing these away. Take a look at how many photographs adorn your walls or surfaces. Sometimes photographs can keep us locked into a past state of mind by acting as reminders of who we once were or those we once knew. Instead of focusing on the here and now and the potential life offers us, too many photographs can keep people trapped into living in the past.

Look carefully and mindfully at these photos you have around you. Select only a very small amount that are framed and hold special personal significance. For example, wedding, graduation, school achievements etc. I have three in my living room, three in my bedroom and three in my hall). Get organised and put any of the remaining photos into albums – do not just place them randomly into drawers to sort at a future date – do it now. Act in the present.

If you have a photo in the future which you would like on display, then replace it with one from the past. Remember life is constantly evolving and so are your memories. By living in the present moment, you are creating the worthwhile memories of the future. Lots of photos of the past can keep us locked into a post state, rather than living in the present and having hope in the future. So be mindful about your photos.

Workplace De-Clutter

Just as in the home, you need to be mindful of the space that you work in. Having too much clutter around you will result in mental overload and chaos and ultimately a decreased productivity. To be productive in work look at what you can control within your immediate environment (especially if you work for an employer). If you are self-employed, work alone or from home this is obviously far easier to achieve. If you have a desk, ensure it is a clear space, file any excessive papers, books, pens etc. Avoid having multiple items on your walls. Keep them as clear as possible to enable you to focus. Many people often have photographs on their desks of loved ones. Again, keep these to an absolute minimum, so that you are fully present in your work, rather than missing children or pets at home, or wishing you were with your partner etc. Any photos you place around you should act as a source of motivation in your work rather than a distraction. Having a declutter can reduce stress and improve mental capacity which will then result in improved productivity in your job (McMains and Kastner, 2011). So, clear the clutter at work and focus mindfully on the task at hand.

Mindful Shopping

If you have followed the above principles of mindful de-cluttering, do you really want to re-stock your home again by shopping? No. So, there are some basic rules to follow to become more mindful when you shop.

However, firstly it is important to outline why shopping is not always either a mundane or pleasurable experience. According to the UK charity UK-Rehab, shopping addiction (like many other addictions) is often a masking agent for under lying conditions like anxiety or depression. It is suggested that like other behavioural addictions it is deep rooted and is characterised by an overwhelming compulsion to make new purchases constantly, whether you need them or not.

Several studies have been cited that suggest that approximately 3% of adults and 8% of young people in Europe and around 2% to 12% of people in the US have symptoms consistent with shopping addiction and compulsive buying (UK-Rehab, 2021).

Shopping is a vital part of life which is inescapable, so learning how to be mindful when shopping can really help tackle to urge for compulsive purchasing and buying yet more things that you will never need.

Being present fully in the moment when you shop is crucial so that you avoid purchasing things you do not need.

Avoid the temptation to shop online and always aim to shop physically in a shop. The reason is that you are more likely to make an instantaneous purchase online whereby you give in to a compulsive purchase without fully considering it.

Aim to shop physically. However, if you cannot then give yourself the following rules to stick by which work mindfully in both physical and online shops:

1) **Is this purchase necessary?**
2) **Do I need it?**
3) **Will I use it?**
4) **When will I use it?**
5) **Can I afford it?**
6) **How will it enhance my life?**
7) **Can I live without it?**

Take your time and then walk away for 15 minutes. If you have answered all of the above questions and fully immersed yourself mindfully in the process, then see how you now feel about your purchase.

Now, another thing about hoarders and compulsive shoppers is the number of items that are collected from sales, which never either get worn or used. If you have completed the de-cluttering exercise above, then you will have the proof! So how can you avoid the urge to splurge the cash in the sales? There is a simple mindful trick. If you spot a bargain, ask yourself the above questions. However, now ask yourself this vital question:

'If this item was full price, would I buy it?'

If the answer is "no" then walk away. Never buy anything just because it is cheap or appears good value for money. Only buy things that you need and that will enhance your life. This is especially true for clothes, because the compulsion to purchase cheap clothes can often be all consuming, yet often these bargains are not purchased because you actually want them but because you think it is a bargain and often because you think that if you do not buy it then someone else will see it and you will miss out! What you are doing is living your life in a fast forward mode – almost as though you are in a low grade "fight or flight" response. Notice the physical symptoms you feel when you are about to make that compulsive and unnecessary purchase. Pay attention to your breathing and heart rate. Often the stress response is triggered and the compulsion to act "quickly" becomes an overwhelming urge, just as in the fight or flight response. Therefore, it is essential to be mindful and fully present when you shop and to take your time by engaging in the shopping process.

Shopping for groceries is another "danger area" and one that really can be helped by becoming more mindful.

1) Before shopping always check your cupboards to see what you need and what you already have.
2) Make a list of what you need.
3) Plan which meals you will be cooking and what is required based on what you already have and require.
4) Never shop when you are hungry! Always shop on a full stomach so that hunger is not a distraction and a trigger to buy more than you need.
5) Take the list with you and only purchase what is on it.

6) Do not get sucked into the temptation of sales items or offers (i.e., buy one get one free). Remember how you decluttered your cupboards and how much out of date products that were never used! Food waste in the West is one of the biggest offenders in terms of household waste.

7) Never buy anything "just in case." Live in the present moment.

8) If you are feeling down, become aware of your mood and recognise it mindfully (remember the earlier mindful metaphors like "thoughts as clouds" etc.) and avoid the shops. Take yourself off to exercise instead. It will improve your mood far more than the thrill of shopping. Your mood is a temporary state.

The guiding principle of mindful shopping is to be present fully in the moment and to make considered purchases only for the things you truly want or need. Never buy anything "just in case." By becoming more mindful when you shop, you will be living a more fulfilled life in the present, and also you will be financially better off too!

Remember this:

'A dead man's cupboards are full of unused stuff and uneaten foods.'

Mindful Laughter

'As soap is to the body, so laughter is to the soul.'
(Jewish Proverb)

There is no better way of placing yourself within the present moment than mindful laughter. When we laugh, we bring out the true nature of our child-like playful self. However, the psychological, physiological, social, emotional, and spiritual aspects of laughter cannot be overstated enough. In short, laughter is one of the best medicines there is, and there is a lot of emerging research to support its use in therapy.

However, in terms of the "M" within the REMIND approach, mindful laughter deserves almost a chapter (if not a book) within its own right.

Dr Madan Kataria is a medical doctor who first brought to the world's attention the therapeutic benefits of combining yoga exercises with laughter. He is often referred to as the "Guru of Giggling." He went on to found "laughter clubs" and established laughter yoga.

In his book, *Laughter Yoga – Daily Practices For Health and Happiness* (Kataria, 2020), he cites two models of laughter:

   i.   Adult or Humour Model.
   ii. Childlike Model or Body-Mind Model.

Adult Model

The first model or the adult model is dependent upon humour and our interpretation of what we find funny. It is dependent upon a whole range of cognitive processes and external stimuli. It differs between person to person (so you may not find the same thing as funny as another person etc.). For example, it is unlikely that if you hear a joke a second time then you will not laugh as much as you did the first-time round.

Childlike Model

Now this is where laughter gets really interesting in terms of mindfulness. The next time you see a child, pay very careful attention to the way in which they laugh. They laugh most when they are playing. So, in other words when they are fully focused on being in the present moment. Laughter is spontaneous and they do not think "too hard" about what makes them laugh. They just do it. Dr Katria believes that this ability to laugh is innate. It is within us. We are literally born with the ability to laugh, but as we become older, we lose this spontaneous inner laughter. One of the features of this sort of laughter is active participation and this is a key feature of mindfulness by fully immersing yourself without judgement in a humorous or fun activity like play, singing/dancing etc. Anything that gives you pleasure is likely to trigger off a laughter and joy response if you are fully immersing yourself mindfully.

It is about re-claiming that childlike playfulness and curiosity about the world that will prompt that inner child to laugh more. There is a big difference between being "funny" and having fun. It is the having fun that connects most closely to mindfulness. Playful laughter stimulates the inner child within all of us.

Fake Laughter in Mindfulness

What is so interesting is that faking laughter often leads to the real thing. In fact, fake laughter stimulates the same regions of the brain that genuine spontaneous laughter does. Even if you are feeling depressed, practicing fake laughter can raise mood significantly.

A further note of importance is that you can literally re-train your brain so that it is more receptive to laughter, and it becomes a spontaneous behavioural response.

For example, in the first chapter we covered the importance of routine within the REMIND approach ("R"). Now what I always advocate in my clients is to get up and shower/ bathe as soon as they wake. What we also know is that the morning is the best time to begin to establish any new patterns of behaviour (before the day begins and you start to procrastinate). So, why not build fake laughter into your daily showering and bathing routine? You will be fulfilling several key aspects all at once.

Many people feel self-conscious when they first begin to practice mindful fake laughter. So, to begin with it is easier if you do so in private. Where better than to do so in the privacy of your own bathroom? In fact, Dr Kataria, promotes the practice himself. He believes that with practice it becomes a conditioned response (rather like the famous experiment involving Pavlov's dogs where they would salivate at the sound of the bell – even in absence of food because food had been brought to them when a bell rang). So, with practice you can learn to laugh spontaneously when you shower, whilst immersing yourself in the mindful process of bathing. A double hit! Try to use a 40-day formula. This means that it takes around 40 days before any new skill becomes a habit. Laughter is no different.

Getting Started with Mindful Laughter

Breathe

Practice your breathing. Breathing is also a key component of mindful meditation. When we laugh, we provide our hearts and lungs with an excellent cardiovascular workout. So, start with learning deep breathing exercises.

The key thing with breathing is to slow it down. Inhale (breathe in) through the nose then exhale (breathe out) through the mouth. The exhalations should be longer than the inhalations so that you get rid of the "stale residual air" which is stored within the lungs as you breathe out. Keep practicing this simple method and what you will notice is that your tummy starts to move in an upwards direction. This is how we know we are breathing correctly and deeply. It is our diaphragm pushing our lungs upwards to help expel the stale air from the lungs and to make way for new fresh oxygen rich fresh air to enter.

This breathing technique also helps you to calm down when you feel anxious, so keep practicing it. Slow deep breaths. Breathe out longer than you breathe in. Stress and depression cause your breathing to become shallow and irregular so that there is a build-up of carbon dioxide. Deep breathing helps to replenish the body with much needed mood busting oxygen.

The next time you laugh pay close attention to the way in which you breathe. You exhale far longer than you do whilst laughing than when you are not laughing. So, prepare your body for laughter by learning how to mindfully breathe.

Smile

All laughter begins with a smile. So, begin by practicing smiling. Hold the smile. Notice how your face feels. Pay attention to your facial muscles. Look in a mirror whilst smiling and study your smile as it is reflected back at you. How does it make you feel?

Now pay careful attention to your eyes. When we are genuinely smiling it is reflected at us via our eyes. You do not simply smile with your mouth but with your eyes too. It is one of the reasons that why, during the Covid Pandemic (whilst wearing masks) we knew who was smiling at us – despite not seeing their mouths. So, smile fully. Your eyes should have little lines at either side and appear to be being pushed upwards whilst smiling fully.

Smile kindly and compassionately at yourself. Treat yourself with the kindness that you would treat a sick friend or relative. Smile genuinely at yourself and notice how smiling makes you feel.

Clap and Laugh

Now start clapping and smiling. Focus mindfully on your clapping. Feel how your hands feels. Did you know that by clapping you are also stimulating your brain's ability to place you in the "here and now" by facilitating proprioception, which acts to calm you down? In traditional Eastern Medicine, the clapping action also helps to stimulate energy levels by activating the acupressure points in the hands. So, clapping will not only calm you it will also help to raise positive energy levels at the same time as being mindful.

Dr Kataria suggests that whilst clapping you begin with a simple chant of "ho, ho" and "ha, ha, ha" which is repeated constantly. He uses this process as a foundation for his laughter yoga.

Practice different sounds whilst laughing. Notice which parts of the body are stimulated whilst doing the laughter exercises. For example, the "ho, ho" sounds tend to be felt in the belly area, whilst the "he, he, he" sounds are mostly felt in the throat.

Once you have mastered this, experiment with your laughter. Practice giggling and silent laughter. The important thing is to try and connect with your child-like self, whilst being mindful in the present moment. Keep faking it until it becomes genuine laughter. With any new skill practice makes perfect and laughing is no exception within mindfulness. We will discuss laughter again when we cover the "I" of the

REMIND approach (Invest in self and others) as it is such a core component in terms of wellbeing.

Case Study

Robert

Robert is a 30-year-old chef who worked in a care home. Robert was experiencing severe health anxiety. He felt that it had been exacerbated as the care home was for elderly people, many of whom were either extremely ill or disabled. He found that his thoughts were constantly being dominated about his own health and his eventual death. Even though he was a young man, seeing so much ill health around him acted as a trigger to force his thinking about possible future illnesses.

Robert stated that every time he felt the slightest twinge, he was convinced it was a stroke, or a headache turned into a brain tumour. He would then start to think about how he would die in a terrible way. His doctor had run multiple medical tests which were all negative and had tried his best to reassure Robert that he was fit and well – only for him to develop a "new" symptom every time.

In the end Robert had to take time off with stress from his job.

One of the most effective strategies to help him cope with managing his anxiety was mindfulness. Robert never lived fully in the present moment as he was so concerned about what was going to happen to him in the future. Even when Robert was on holiday or having a meal out, he could never fully enjoy these experiences as he was never fully present.

What he found to be effective, was building in sensory mindfulness so instead of him perceiving normal bodily sensations as potential terminal illnesses he could see how they were just part of everyday life and that they would pass. But most importantly, he learnt how to enjoy sensory experiences, like food (after all he was a chef), exercise, nature etc. in real time as they happened in the present. We also built more laughter into his mindful routine to keep him focused on the joy and fun of life, rather than death. In doing so, mindfulness helped him to live a life worth leading in the present, rather than in the future.

Summary

This chapter has outlined some basic ways of building and becoming more mindful in your everyday life. Try to lead a simple life and learn how live fully in the present moment. De clutter any excessive items. Keep practicing and try to become more mindful to live and experience life more fully. Build mindfulness into all you do. It should become a natural seamless part of your routine, so that it is incorporated into exercise, investing in yourself and others, within nature and obviously your diet too (especially mindful eating). Being present and living your life completely in the moment is an essential component of the REMIND approach and with practice it can become second nature in leading a life worth living, being fulfilled and happier too. Laugh often, in a mindful way.

Chapter 4
I = Invest in Self and
Others – Self

So, the "I" in the REMIND approach stands for "Invest in self and others." However, before you can invest in another person it is vital that you can firstly invest in yourself. For this reason, this chapter will be devoted to the self, whilst the following one, will cover how we can invest in other people.

Be Kind to Yourself.
'You cannot pour from an empty cup.'

Firstly (and most importantly), you need to treat yourself with kindness. Most people, put themselves last in life. They feel that other people are somehow more deserving of kindness, compassion, and appreciation than themselves. So here are some very practical things you can do right now in terms of immediately boosting your own self-care:

Never save your "best items" for a more "deserving" time or event in the future. If you have a favourite item of clothing which you never wear as it is too "good", then get it out of your wardrobe right now and put it on. The same goes for your favourite perfume, body lotion, soap, deodorant, aftershave etc., etc. Never, leave them in the future, because you must start living in the present moment, which is now. Not in ten years' time. It must start right now.

The same principle applies to how you eat your meals. If you have good crockery, glass ware, cups etc. Use them now and make every mealtime occasion a time to celebrate (even if you are just having beans on toast with a glass of water). How you present and serve food really matters (we will discuss this further in the chapter covering "Diet" in the REMIND Approach).

Change How You View Yourself

Common Negative Chatter

It is very, very common when people enter therapy (and remember anyone who enters therapy is extremely courageous) that there has been a long period of "unkindness" to themselves. For example, continuous negative self-thought and inner distress and turmoil. Here are some common thoughts that people often have about themselves:

'I don't deserve to be happy.'
'I am not good enough.'
'I hate how I look.'
'I can`t cope.'
'I am a failure.'
'Everybody is better than me.'
'I will never find love.'
'I can't get a job I like.'

'Everyone is mean to me.'
'There must be something wrong with me.'
'I'm ugly.'
'I always fail at everything.'

The above list could go on and on. In fact, I could probably fill an entire book with all the negative self-talk that people constantly repeat to me about how they feel. Now, do you think you are treating yourself with kindness by repeating these thoughts to yourself? Your answer may well be something like "I don't know how to be happy", "I don't know how to stop" etc. Right, well let's look again at that very long list, only this time I want you to imagine you are saying those things to a vulnerable person at their lowest ebb:

'You don't deserve to be happy.'
'You are not good enough.'
'I hate how you look.'
'You can't cope.'
'You are a failure.'
'Everybody is better than you.'
'You will never find love.'
'You can't get a job you like.'
'Everyone is mean to you.'
'There must be something wrong with you.'
'You are ugly.'
'You always fail at everything.'

I expect you do not feel very comfortable saying those dreadful things to a vulnerable person who is at breaking point. You probably think that only the worst sort of bully could ever say such terrible things to a person in distress? Yes, you are right. So now you know how unkind you have been treating your own self, and why when you think such dreadful things, they make you feel so unhappy.

Remember, as humans we are programmed to have a negative bias, so that we are more likely to pay attention to negative thoughts than positive ones. It links to the primitive "fight or flight" response so that we can perceive danger. However, what happens with constant negative self-talk is that it merely keeps us trapped in a circle of destructive thinking, so it becomes almost impossible to pay attention to positive (and more realistic) ways of being.

'You should treat yourself with the same love and care that you would give to a sick relative or friend.'

I use the above saying all the time with my own clients It is quite amazing how cruel we are to our own selves in times of crisis and despair. We can all benefit from kindness and compassion. You would not say any of the above to a sick relative or friend, so why do it to yourself?

However, words in themselves do not contain emotions. It is meaning that we place upon them and how we both interpret and use words that allows them to contain the feelings (which then feed into how we feel about ourselves). They are not facts.

Flick the Switch to Be Kind to Yourself

It is vital to be able to recognise when you are using the negative self-chatter and to be able to have the control and ability to stop. Re-claiming your power over how you choose to think and speak to yourself is a core component of developing a healthy and more hopeful state of mind. If we look at the above lists, we can see how to simply replace and change those statements so that they can be directed towards someone who is vulnerable or sick:

'You deserve to be happy.'
'You are good enough.'
'I like how you look.'
'You can cope.'
'You are not a failure.'
'You are as good as anyone else.'
'You will find love.'
'You can get a job you like.'
'Most people are kind.'
'You are perfect as you are.'
'You are beautiful.'
'You can succeed.'

Saying the above statements to someone who is vulnerable, probably feels a lot more comfortable. Most people do not like to say deliberately hurtful things to another person and cause them distress or pain. It is not in our human nature.

Now I want you to go back over the above set of statements and say them out loud. Imagine you are saying them to someone you know who is sick or in need of help. If you have a photo of them even better, place it in front. Say the above statements loudly and keep repeating them as though you can see that person and you want to convince them. They might not believe you, but it is your mission to make them see all the good qualities that are inside of them. You want to make them see how much you value them. How does it feel?

Re-claim Power over Your Thoughts

Seeing Yourself Activity

The next part of this kindness exercise is to use powerful self-love affirmations directly to yourself.

It helps if you sit in front of the mirror so that you can use your reflection as the "other person" in need. This is quite powerful as you are speaking directly to your reflection and seeing yourself as you are – a person who is worthy of kindness and compassion.

Alternatively, try to find a photo of your much younger self as a child. This in fact links to another form of therapy called "Inner child work" and this exercise can be adapted to reach the innocent, hopeful qualities that exist in all of us.

However, if you feel unable to look at yourself as a child, or as an adult in the mirror, just now (or do not feel fully comfortable with this), then simply write your name down on a piece of paper and try saying the following self-love affirmations out loud. Say them like you mean them and repeat them over and over.

'I deserve happiness.'
'I love you (Insert your own name here).'
'I am good enough.'
'I can cope.'
'I am a success.'
'I am as good as anyone else.'
'I will find love.'
'I can get a job I like.'
'I am perfect as I am.'
'I am beautiful.'
'I can succeed.'

Keep working at the above. Choose one or two of the positive self-talk affirmations that resonate with your situation right now. Pick something that you want to improve in your life (remember the SMART goals from the first chapter of the REMIND approach) and keep repeating your statement (or affirmation). Have these written down so that you can access them throughout the day (especially at times when negative thoughts might creep in).

Meditation for Self-Kindness

This is a very simple, yet effective, meditation exercise which I frequently teach my own clients:

Begin by sitting comfortably, support your back if needed with cushions, place your feet on the floor and have your palms gently resting on your lap in front of you. Close your eyes.

Focus on your breathing (see the chapter on mindfulness for a good breathing exercise).

Breathe in through your nose and out through your mouth.

Slow your breathing right down and spend more time exhaling than inhaling (this is very important).

You will notice as your breathing becomes slower and deeper that your stomach area should gently rise and fall as you begin to use more of your lung capacity.

If unwanted thoughts come into your head, just view them as clouds passing across a sky and do know judge them. Allow them to pass and refocus your attention back to your slow, deep gentle breaths in and out.

Once you have established this, then focus all your attention on your heart.

Imagine a golden light entering your heart with every breath you breathe in, bringing with it feelings of love and kindness.

Focus all your attention on these feelings of love and kindness and slowly allow them to spread outwards so that they start to fill your whole being.

Next allow yourself to experience all the feelings of love and kindness as if you were a "deserving child." This is especially important if you did not receive kindness as a child. Allow yourself to feel the kindness and to feel deserving of the kindness. Because no matter what has happened in the past you truly are deserving of kindness right now.

Allow yourself to bask in this feeling of love and kindness. Allow yourself to feel deserving of this kindness and of love.

As you breathe in imagine more kindness and love entering your body.

As you breathe out, allow all the pain and sadness of the past to leave your body, making way for more kindness and love to enter your body with every breath you inhale.

Give yourself the permission to feel love and kindness.

When you are ready, bring yourself back and slowly open your eyes.

Now say out loud:

'I am worthy of love and kindness.'

This is a simple, yet profoundly healing exercise for bringing more kindness and love into your life. Try to build this simple exercise into your daily routine so that you can start to build a more compassionate and kinder relationship with yourself.

Forming New Positive Paths

Remember, as humans we are programmed to have a negative bias. Therefore, you need to retrain your brain so that you forge more positive neural pathways within it. Negative thinking patterns are often well-established and ingrained in people. However, the good news is, that the brain loves to form new pathways. In fact, we know that the brain undergoes neuroplastic changes throughout life. Even in traumatic brain injuries other areas of the brain change and take over functions. So, at a cognitive level we can re-train how we think so we become not only more positive but also far kinder on ourselves and responsive to opportunities of life around us.

Imagine you are in a field of long grass, to the side of you there is a well-trodden pathway where the grass has been walked upon many times. You can see a pathway within the grass that has been so well-used that the earth beneath is showing. This pathway only leads to a muddy bog, where the sun never shines, that holds no pleasure. It is a dark, dank place. You are not even sure why people choose to walk down there.

However, in front of you, you can see long grass and if you walk through it, then you will form a new pathway which, with time, will also become a well-trodden path within the field. At the end you can see a field of beautiful flowers, where the sun is shining, a wonderful perfume scent fills the air. You feel hopeful that something nice awaits. However, the grass to get there is long and it looks like no one has ever walked it. What you do know is that the well-trodden path to your side does not lead to an enjoyable place, but the grass ahead does.

You now have a choice. Will you choose to walk the well-trodden path once again to the familiar place that holds no pleasure? Or will you choose to form a new pathway through the long grass to the beautiful place, which can become a well-used route, full of new and exciting experiences?

The path that already exists to your side in the field represents the well-trodden, negative neural thought pathway, which you have used thousands of times before in your brain. It represents all those constant dreadful thoughts you have about yourself which you think repeatedly. However, the untrodden long grass ahead of you represents a new way of thinking about yourself. It represents a positive and more productive way of thinking. If you choose the route ahead, you will be forging a new positive neural thought network in your brain. Once you forge a positive neural network, it then, like the new path ahead of you becomes easier to tread each time you choose to walk it.

So, to make this exercise easier, I will take one of our statements from the previous lists.

"I am a failure" represents the negative self-talk thought pattern which is your well-trodden path to your side within the field.

"I can succeed" represents positive (and more realistic) self-talk thought pattern, which is the long grass ahead of you where you can forge a new path to new and exciting opportunities.

Keep practicing this exercise. The more you do it the easier the path becomes.

Passion in Life

Find your passion in life. Find what you LOVE to do. This can be either via your work or your hobbies but find something that really makes your heart sing. Invest in yourself so that you find your true vocation in life or the hobby that will give you the happiness you deserve. It is the thing that makes you passionate and hopeful, and these feed into your sense of self and identity.

Many people never take the time out, to discover their passion, and sadly often, this can be the reason why so few feel truly fulfilled in life. Whatever your own meaning and purpose in life is, it can always be discovered. It already lies within you. You just need to discover it. So, take the time to invest in yourself to find it.

We will discuss why it is vital to find the "job" that gives you fulfilment, because work is an inescapable part of life. You need money to live, but often work is one of the major sources of stress and dissatisfaction for people. It is also one of the biggest barriers in preventing you from discovering your true purpose and passion in life too.

Work

'Play is the child's work.'
(Original author of this concept is unknown)

The above is an extremely famous, and well used, quotation. It has been credited to numerous pioneers of children's rights, education, philosophy, and developmental psychology over the centuries. If you conduct an internet search on who first developed this phrase you will find lots of opposing results. My interpretation of the meaning is not that play is an excuse not to work as adults do, rather that we learn valuable life lessons through play. Adults have a lot to learn about the purpose of child-like play.

Play is not merely about having fun (although it is fun too) but it serves a very important purpose in terms of later adult work. Through play, children learn valuable new resources, enhance problem solving abilities and develop social skills in a highly vital and productive way. It is through play that children learn resilience and persistence, experimenting through trial and error. As children, we constantly make sense of the world around us and the consequences of our actions through both solitary and shared play.

One of the most crucial (and often overlooked aspects of play) is that children learn what their abilities and passions are. So, in other words, what their unique talents in life are and their place in the world.

Some of the most contented and fulfilled people in life have never lost this connection to the child-like wonder of play. Their so called "hobbies" and interests from childhood have transferred over in later life to what they chose to do as a job or profession. They have a high degree of job satisfaction because they were allowed to follow their passion in life. So, their "job" is not just a means to make money, pay the bills and get by in life. No, their job is an inextricable part of their identity. It is something they would continue to do even if they were not paid. So, work for them is their "play."

'Work Is the Adult's Play'

So, I have taken the famous quotation of "Play is the child's work" and rephrased it to the above. If you both enjoy and feel a passion for what you do in life, work can become the "play" of an adult's life in the same way as it acts in that of children.

PERMA Theory

Interestingly, work that is linked to being your true vocation will bring you a greater sense of happiness and well-being. One of the founders of positive psychology Martin Seligman (Seligman, 2012) outlines a model which can be used as a framework for being happy at work and leading a fulfilling life. This is known as the PERMA theory. It stands for:

Positive emotion (feeling happy or content with everyday tasks)

Engagement (so tasks that you find both interesting and challenge you)

Meaning (finding your true purpose)

Relationships (feeling connected to others)

Achievement (finding out and being good at something)

Break the Cycle of Job Dissatisfaction

A major reason why people seek therapy is dissatisfaction with their work and careers. Not feeling fulfilled or even being on the "right path" (as I frequently hear it being called) can make people feel as though they are just "existing" and not "living." Most people, live from pay-cheque to pay-cheque on a monthly or weekly basis. They feel stuck in jobs because of their financial responsibilities and barely earn enough to pay the bills at times. On days off they frequently worry about having to return to work. They do not appear to live life fully in the moment when enjoyable opportunities arise.

One way to break this cycle psychologically is to take and long and honest look at your reasons for working in the job you do and why you do so. This may seem like an obvious start, but it is rarely something that many people have ever given their full attention to (especially those who feel stuck or trapped in their current employment).

My True Vocation Activity

We know that people who treat work as a vocation are far happier and more content in general. So, if you are feeling particularly trapped in your job now, I want you to complete the following exercise which I developed for my own clients:

Start by placing your name followed by the following sentence:

I (name) work as (then place your job title here)

Now list all the things that you ENJOY about your job.

I always start the enjoyment part first. The reason is, because your brain has told you a million times over the reasons why you "hate" your job, your boss, your colleagues etc. But very rarely have you considered the positive aspects of work. Therefore, it is important to start the exercise by beginning firstly with the positive aspects, or the things you like about your job. Now consider these carefully. They may be small things like being able to be flexible, you may like the walk into work, you may like the fact there are good shops to browse in or sights to see on your journey in. You may even like the fact that there are one or two people you like in your place of work. The trick is to try and think in more wider terms about the positive aspects of your job. Anything at all positive that you associate with your job is fine to put on your list. Of course, do not forget the primary reason why we all work: money.

It is important that you spend some time really considering every aspect.

Now list all the things that you DISLIKE about your job.

I do not need to give specific examples here, as I am sure that you can think of plenty of reasons of your own. However, the common ones I hear most of in therapy are bullying, lack of fulfilment, lack of acknowledgement and feeling trapped.

When we are very focused on all the negative aspects of a job, it is almost impossible to see the original reasons why you both applied and took the job you are in, in the first place.

So next, I want you to list all the reasons why you applied for your job in the first place.

You can include as many reasons as you so wish. Anything that you feel might be the original reasons. For example, it was local, it was flexible, it suited your family/ caring commitments, it was a good source of income, you would meet new people, etc., etc.

Now, if you did not include "I could use my skills" in your reasons for applying for the job, I want you to do so now. Think back to what your original skills were at the time and how they were matched to your current job.

Next list all the skills that you have that make you employable.

Now I want you to make a list of all the things that you REALLY ENJOY doing outside of work. For example, hobbies, interests etc. as an adult. If you currently do not have time to do the things you want to do, then list all the things that you would enjoy if you had more time to do so.

Think back to the time when you were a child, what were the sorts of things that you enjoyed doing? What games did you like? What interests did you have? If you were denied from doing certain activities as a child, what would have been the kinds of things you would have like to try or do? Now make a list.

So now you should have lots of lists in front of you. Briefly you should be able to see a pattern emerging in terms of **likes, skills, and challenges** to overcome.

Next, I want you to consider the sorts of **different jobs that you can do** based on the things you liked as a child (or even what you would have liked as a child if given the opportunity), what you like as an adult, what you enjoy about your current job and finally what you do not like in your current job. The latter bit is very telling as it gives you an indication of the sorts of work/ situations to avoid in the future.

Now make a list of alternative jobs you could do. Look at your current skills and likes. Do you need to do more training etc. to do your dream job, or could you do it now?

Next, I want you to visualise yourself fully in your dream job being at this exact moment in time. Everything about the job, including anyone you may work with, the sorts of the things you do etc., etc.

I want you to write your name and your new job title:
I (name) work as a (place the job title here)

Now I want you to list all the things you like about this job.

Next, I want you to list all the things you dislike about this job (if indeed there are any negative aspects to it)

Now how do you feel if you fully allow yourself to be capable of being in the job you deserve and want? Do you feel good? Do you feel satisfied with work? Do you feel like you are fulfilling your potential in life?

Now consider this interesting concept in relation to your current position and the job you do not like at present. You have a choice:

1) *Stay exactly as you are and do not change anything about your current situation. Remember not changing is the same as taking action to leave, because what you are saying is by staying is "I am fine as I am."*

2) Or do you put in place the steps and processes to make the changes needed to lead a more fulfilling life?

At the end of this exercise, you should have the overall answer to your predicament, plus some valuable and positive insights into realistic work alternatives. You should always aim to work in a job that feels like "play" to a child. So, in other words, a job that makes you feel as fulfilled as you did when you engaged in the occupation of play as a child. A job should also ensure you feel valued, and you are making a unique contribution. A job that you are truly fulfilling your potential in life whilst doing.

One way to simply assess if you are fulfilling your potential in life is by answering this simple question:

'If you won the Lottery tomorrow and money was no object, would you still work?'

"Job Like a Student"

One way to change how you mentally view your current job is to view it as a temporary situation. A temporary role in which you are gaining the money needed to provide the means for you to work towards gaining your "dream job." I call this 'Job like a Student.'

What this means is to totally change how you psychologically view your current job situation, so the only focus is money. This is in the same way that college and university students, take on menial jobs to help pay their way, whilst studying for their true vocation. Many students do a whole range of different jobs alongside their studies. However, the focus of their attention is not the job they do to pay their way but rather the end goal of achieving their degree and entering their chosen profession.

If you can mentally approach your current job, in which you may feel stuck or unhappy, as being a temporary situation, that serves a purpose, it helps immensely in instilling hope. Hope is the positive innate drive which gives us choice and opportunities in life. When people feel they have no hope, they feel they have no choice but to remain in jobs, or situations that cause them distress. So, in terms of your work. Find your passion, focus on your goal, and view your current job like a student. You have hope, so invest in yourself.

Work Affirmations

'I am grateful for the opportunity of work.'
'My job provides me with the money to do enjoyable things.'
'I enjoy working towards achieving my goals.'
'I am grateful for the ability to work.'
'Work provides me with purpose and meaning.'

Laugh More

Laughter literally is one of the best medicines in terms of psychological wellbeing. So, if you are going to invest in yourself, then make a note to build laughter into a regular routine. One of the main benefits is because when we laugh it releases mood boosting endorphins into the body which help to give us a natural high. Laughter affects mood, so you get instant feedback that you feel much better within, when you have a good laugh. We covered mindful laughter in our chapter on Mindfulness ("M" in the REMIND approach).

However, there is much scientific evidence to support the fact that laughter not just helps to release feel good chemicals which make us feel happier but there are wider health benefits too. A study from Japan in 2019, by Dr Yoshikawa and colleagues focused on providing laughter therapy in a day centre for elderly patients. All the participants had impaired cognitive function and physical difficulties which resulted in them having poor activities of daily living. They found some quite incredible results in terms of, not just the psychological benefits of laughter but also the physical effects on health too. They found that laughter helped to reduce blood pressure and heart rate in the patients. This was also accompanied by a significant increase in serotonin (which boosts mood). They found there was a significant decrease in depression and that sociability increased too. In addition to this they found that activity levels increased following laughter therapy. Their conclusion to their study recommended that laughter therapy should be prescribed alongside other standard medical interventions to help boost overall quality of life (Yoshikawa et al., 2019).

How to Invest in Laughter Right Now

So, if you are reading this and you need more laughter then there are some practical tips to invest in yourself.

Start by smiling. Smile right now. Focus on how it feels in your face and hold the position for longer and longer each time. Smiling is the first step towards laughing.

Keep a laughter diary. The reason behind a laughter diary, you can then find the sorts of things that amuse you. It also reinforces that life has opportunities for laughter (not just sadness).

Make it a point of watching comedies on TV. Avoid anything which may act as a trigger to make your feel sad. Find what makes you laugh and invest in it. Make it a mission to bring laughter into your life by researching the sorts of humour you like to watch on television then actively seek it out.

Investigate joining a laughter therapy group (either online or in person). One aspect of laughter therapy is the use of fake laughter. Yes, you read that right, faking laughter. Aayushi Kapoor in 2021, suggests that faking laughter can turn into real laughter with all the associated benefits (Kapoor, 2021).
There is also a growing trend of laughter yoga (as outlined in our section on Mindfulness). This combines, the

traditional mind, body, and spiritual elements of traditional yoga with the use of laughter. It is often referred to as Hasya Yoga and was started by Dr Madan Kataria (Kataria, 2020) and focuses on breathing techniques to stimulate laughter whilst stretching. Consider finding an online group (you will also be fulfilling the "E", "M" and "I" here within the REMIND approach.

Overall, whatever you do invest in yourself by bringing more laughter into your everyday life.

Here are some jokes to cheer you up right now:

"Did you hear about the cockle who went to the seafood disco? She pulled a mussel."

"How did Darth Vader know what Luke had bought him for Christmas? He felt his presents."

"Last week I went to the zoo, and I only saw one dog in it. It was a shih tzu."

"My dog used to chase people on a bike a lot. It got so bad I had to take the bike off him."

"I went to visit my doctor." I said, "Doctor I can't stop singing the 'Green, Green Grass of Home.'"
The Doctor said, "That sounds like Tom Jones Syndrome."
I said, "How common is it?"
He said, "It's not unusual."

Laughter Affirmations.
'I love to laugh.'
'Laughter is my joy.'
'Life has opportunities for laughter and fun.'

Learn More

'Learn from yesterday, live for today, hope for tomorrow. The important thing is to not stop questioning.'
(Albert Einstein)

Invest in yourself by learning more. Life is a journey for learning. We are not just meaning the sorts of learning associated with college or school but everyday hobbies, skills, travel…discover your passion in life by learning. Learning new things and being naturally curious (like a child does) provides the hope and motivation to live a life worth living.

It is interesting that our brains seem to expand when we feel better. So, a positive mood has a direct effect on cognitive processing. Back in 2010, a team from The University of Western Ontario, by Ruby Nadler and colleagues, conducted research which demonstrated how a positive mood can really impact upon our ability to learn new knowledge (Nadler et al., 2010).

However, one thing that learning new knowledge or skills does is, it provides a sense of accomplishment. It sends a clear signal that not only can you succeed in things, but you can also enjoy the process of learning too. So, it feeds into our overall sense of self-worth and self-efficacy. In short, we learn what we CAN do.

So, try to build the process of learning as a fun and enjoyable activity as much as possible into the REMIND approach. Invest in yourself by learning something new each day (even if it is a new word from the Dictionary or a new television show). Expanding your knowledge for fun will make you feel better.

Learning Affirmations:
'I enjoy learning new skills.'
'I enjoy learning new knowledge.'
'I deserve learning new things.'
'Learning discovers my talents.'

The Power of Visualisation

'Visualisation is more important than knowledge.'
(Albert Einstein)

Once you know what it is you want to achieve then you need to put the process into action. In chapter one, we covered the concept of setting SMART goals which are often used in CBT. However, you always need to have the end goal in sight. An effective way of creating a positive mindset is through visualisation. Imagining that you have already achieved your goal is a very good way of "tricking" the brain. Interestingly the brain has difficulty in discerning between reality and non-reality, so visualising success can really help to create a mindset that keeps you motivated and hopeful in the future.

When I was a doctoral student (which is the highest academic qualification in the world), I often had periods when I was filled with self-doubt and worry in terms of whether I would be good enough to succeed. There was no expectation placed upon me to succeed. I came from a deprived background where no one in my immediate family or social circle had ever gone to university, let alone completed a PhD. I had left home aged just 17, so to say it was unusual for someone from my background to go onto gain a doctorate, is an understatement. There were many times when I could have opted for the easy way out and just given up. I had one young baby (my eldest son) when I started and then I had a further baby right in the middle (my daughter). However, I knew I wanted to gain my doctoral degree. It would have been so easy for me to stay at home with my two young children and cease my studies. So, one way of keeping me motivated to succeed and to prevent me from just stopping altogether, was writing my name followed by the letters "PhD." I attained my degree in the minimum time (three years). Not only that but I also became one of the youngest allied health professionals in the United Kingdom at that time to hold both a PhD and a master's degree. All of this whilst working and having a baby right in the middle of my studies. I also won an award for my research and went onto publish my doctoral work in several influential medical and therapy journals.

At that time, I had no idea that what I was doing was using a visualisation technique. I had never at that stage come across this concept. Yet I know for certain that it works. I have since discovered that this is a strategy that many successful people employ. By visualising being successful and how it will feel when you have achieved your goal, not only keeps you motivated to succeed but also focuses your full attention on what it is you truly want in life. The essential thing to do is to focus on the result not the problem(s).

Interestingly, The Law of Attraction is a widely used concept and belief within metaphysical science, religion, and spirituality. It is essentially the Law of Cause and Effect. It is certainly not a new concept and is thought to be thousands of years old and to have been used by several ancient civilisations. Many of the principles can be found in multiple religious and spiritual texts globally. It is by no means a new concept developed for self-help or "new age" therapists. However, the term "Law of Attraction" was first used by Russian author and pioneering Esoteric Philosopher Helena Petrovna Blavatsky in 1877 (Poole, ND).

In basic terms, what you think about has the potential (both good and bad) to be created or manifested. So, the more you think about what you don't want, or don't like, the more of that you will create in your life. The more you think about what you do want, the more likely you are to achieve your goal. The Law of Attraction proposes that you can achieve or have anything that you want in life but you must firstly "give" it to yourself by focusing upon this.

Gratitude is also an important part of helping to establish a positive mindset. Howard Poole in his article about the Law of Attraction (Poole ND) suggests that you can enjoy more positivity in many areas of your life by learning how to be grateful for the things you already have and this in turn helps you to see the world around you far more favourably. In fact, many would consider this to be a key component in positive psychology too.

So, if you want to achieve your goals try visualising achieving them and the steps required to do so. Express your gratitude for all that you have now and look at the opportunities you currently have in your life. In doing so, you will be filled with motivation, hope, optimism and positivity in terms of achieving all that you want in life.

Age Is No Barrier

The physical age you are right now should never deter you from finding your passion in life and investing in yourself. For example, the famous American Star Trek actor William Shatner, went into space for the first time at age 90 in 2021! He is proof that you can achieve your dreams no matter what your physical age is.

Indeed, happiness has a lot to do with the whole process of getting older. One interesting fact is that in life, we start off being happier as very young children and then happiness levels begin to decline. They typically reach a low point around the age of 45 (you may sometimes hear of this being referred to as the "mid-life crisis"). Then after the age of 45 happiness levels begin to improve again, often to the levels of when we were very young! This is great news and something that can provide us with hope as we age.

Yet, despite this promise of getting happier as we become older, age is often seen as the reason why we cannot fulfil our potential in life. A common reason why people produce self-imposed barriers to fulfilling their potential in life, is their physical years. I frequently hear, in therapy, phrases like "Oh I am too old to start again", "I would do it if I was younger",

"It's too late to change now." I must say that typically these sorts of responses are from people aged between 35–50. Stop, just stop! You are not too old to achieve your goals in life or in finding your life's purpose. The sad thing is too many people, never find their true passion but that need not be you, no matter how old you are. Often, people may not be exposed to the experience of what they are good at.

One interesting fact is that older people start to re-prioritise what they can do and place less importance on what they can no longer do, or on materialistic goods. It is about focusing on more meaningful goals, so in other words, the ones that will bring you happiness and enjoyment.

You should always invest in yourself by learning new skills, expanding your knowledge, and developing your innate abilities. Life is for learning. I am going to illustrate this with the following two case studies, both of whom were 80 years young when they found their passion in life.

Case Study

Dave

Dave is a wonderful 80-year-old young man from Liverpool. He was my father's best friend when they were children. Dave has allowed me to share his story, as I am sure it will help others.

At the age of 78 Dave decided he wanted to get fitter. So, he purchased a bike and started going for short rides near his home, along the promenade. As his fitness improved, he started going longer distances and built cycling into his daily routine (an excellent example of the REMIND approach).

He eventually purchased an electric bike so that he could cycle in all weathers (it is often very windy along the seafront where Dave rides). His new bike combined with his improved fitness meant that he took two rides a day in the early morning and late afternoon which totalled 28 miles.

Dave really began to reap both the mental and physical health benefits of cycling and finding his passion in life. Now, the tale does not stop there. Dave eventually joined a local cycling club where he met and made lots of lovely new friends, with whom he could go out for longer social rides each weekend. At the time of writing Dave is 80 and on Sunday he rode his first ever 100-mile cycle ride! Yes, 100 miles in a day at the age of 80. Dave became a cycling "Centurion" at the age of 80. Dave is living proof that you are never too old to find your true passion in life and how to effectively use a REMIND approach by investing in yourself, to aid both mental and physical wellbeing.

Case Study

Ruby

Ruby is my second case study to demonstrate how age is no barrier to discovering your passion in life.

Ruby an 80-year-old woman who had widespread arthritis which affected most of the joints in her body.

When I went to visit Ruby, she answered the door with a huge "beaming smile" to me. I could tell immediately that she was significantly impaired with her arthritis in terms of her general mobility (she used a Zimmer frame to walk with), yet she seemed so "upbeat" and positive. We went through to her sitting room which was full of incredible paintings. She had an easel next to her armchair with fresh paints and a picture she was currently working on.

I naturally assumed she was a life-long artist, so I asked her about her work. Ruby had discovered her innate artistic talent quite by chance several months earlier. Her arthritis in her hands had become so bad that she wanted to do a gentle exercise to keep her hands mobile and to stop them from deteriorating further, so she took up painting. She had never had the opportunity, as a child, to try art due to the second World War, and being evacuated. So, she just assumed she had no natural talent.

She was quite amazed herself at how good her work was. She had discovered her passion. Her newfound ability to paint at the age of 80 had given her life a new meaning and purpose to get up and face life each day. She no longer dreaded the monotony of a lonely day; she now had a reason. Her painting had impacted significantly on her mood and mental wellbeing. Not only that but Ruby also reported less pain in the joints of her hands too.

Ruby is an excellent example of how using a REMIND approach can enhance both mental and physical wellbeing and in finding your true passion in life.

Age Affirmations:
'Age is just a number.'
'Each day I gain more wisdom.'
'I feel younger each day.'
'Age provides me with the chance to try new opportunities.'
'I am improving with age.'

'I am finding my life's true purpose with age.'
Invest Right Now in Yourself.

Invest in Self Affirmations

'Each day bring new hope.'
'I invest in myself the same care I give to others.'
'I have unique gifts.'
'My life purpose is unfolding.'
'I enjoy discovering my talents.'
'I enjoy learning new things.'
'I am thankful for a job to provide money to achieve my passion in life.'
'I enjoy discovering my new interests.'
'Age is no barrier to success.'

Summary

So, we have discussed some of the reasons why it is so vital to place the importance you place on others, firstly onto yourself. You deserve to be happy, and you deserve to lead a life worth living. Never be content to merely exist or to "live" from pay cheque to pay cheque. You are a unique human being with equally unique gifts. You are here for such a short time, and you need to discover your life's purpose and to feel fulfilled. It is never too late to lead the life you have always wanted and to be at peace. The following chapter will now discuss why it is also vital to invest in others alongside yourself and how empathy and kindness can lead to self-actualisation.

Chapter 5
I = Invest in Self and Others – Others

'Whether one believes in religion or not, and whether one believes in rebirth or not, there isn't anyone who doesn't appreciate kindness and compassion.'
(Dalai Lama)

Importance of Investing in Other People

No person can exist solely alone, without interacting with another human ever again. Simply put, it is impossible. We are programmed to be innately social beings who are inter dependent upon others for our basic survival. However, those fellow humans who we should be so connected to, are frequently the same people who are the cause of our emotional pain and distress. So, why should we be seeking even more interaction out? Well, we are certainly not suggesting that you seek out, remain in, or encourage toxic, abusive, or self-destructive relationships, quite the opposite.

During the recent Pandemic, it enforced the need for social contact with other people, when most of the world was placed in enforced lockdown. Isolation, loneliness, and the need for good social relationships were high on many people's agendas.

Equally important, and inextricably linked to the concept of self-care, is investing in others. So, although the previous chapter described the process of how to apply the "I" within yourself, it actually stands for "Invest in self and others."

Being kind, without the expectation of receiving anything in return, is the basis of investing in others.

Importance of Friends

Having friends and social support is vital to our mental and emotional wellbeing. Recent research in 2021 by Peiqi Lu and colleagues from Columbia University in New York investigated the importance of friendship globally and how it links with health and wellbeing. They discovered that friendships could help to enrich life across a variety of settings and contexts (Lu et al., 2021). However, you need the right friends. Not the wrong ones. So, it is vital that you are able to recognise what makes a positive and fulfilling social and emotional relationship. Having the insight will really help you in terms of investing in others and enhancing your own personal relationships with others.

Friendship Activity

Positive and Negative Qualities of Friends

Now I want you to take a moment to consider all the qualities that make your ideal friend. If you currently do not have any friends and are struggling with this part of the book, think about someone you may know who you view as "kind" and would make you a good friend.

I often do a similar activity with my clients and the following words and phrases are very common when describing an "ideal" friend:

Loyalty.
Kindness.
Compassion.
Fun.
Laughter.
Shared Interests.
Always has time for you.
Makes you feel good.
Trustworthy.
Dependable.
Invites you out.
Includes you in their wider social circle.
Feels like family.

The above common words frequently appear during therapy sessions regardless of a person's age, gender, social class, ethnicity, location etc., etc. We all crave the same facets in our friends. However, if you suffer from loneliness, isolation or just seem to "attract" toxic friendships/relationships then the above can just seem like impossible idealisms. Not so. You can attract the sorts of friends you want. So, the reason I deliberately placed the "Invest in self" section before this one covering "Others" is so the process and awareness of how you are begins to transform in a positive way.

Now I want you to consider all the negative aspects that you do not want in a friend. Make a list. I will list some of the common things I hear about during therapy below:

Not loyal.
Not Kind.
"Kind" when they want something from you.
Spiteful.
Selfish.
Puts you down.
Gossip.
Controlling.
Never visits.
Always seems to be doing things without you.
Never invites you.
Jealous.
Untrustworthy.
Never includes you.

So, if we compare the two lists of what people want in their ideal friend and what they do not want, what we can see is a very distinctive pattern emerging. Basically, one list is positive, the other toxic and negative. Well, now you know what you do not want and what you do. That is a good thing surely? However, rather than acting as a "wake up call" what it can do is reinforce that you are surrounding yourself with toxic people.

Relationship De-Clutter

It is important when investing in others, that you are not giving your precious energy to those who are not worthy of it. Although having good friends is vital to our emotional and mental wellbeing, having the wrong sorts of friends or extremely negative ones can be more damaging. For example, research by Rosenquist and colleagues in 2011 found that depression or negative behaviour patterns can be made worse by friends (cited by Lu et. al, 2021). Also, if you have friends who display self-destructive behaviour patterns, then these can subsequently place you also at an increased risk of developing similar traits. Peiqi Lu and colleagues in their work in 2021, cited several earlier studies which demonstrated a link between the risk of obesity, smoking, substance misuse and suicide when you mix with friends or peers who display these traits or behaviours. So having positive people in your life can enhance it but having negative people will not.

Too much energy is spent on people who are exploitative, controlling, or coercive in therapy. It is vital to be able to recognise who is worth investing your time in and who to avoid! So, it is always good to have a "detox" of anyone who is not adding anything positive to your own social and emotional wellbeing.

Firstly, make a list of all the people you have in your life.

Next to each name write a list of **positive** and **negative** aspects of the friendship or relationship.

Now think about a time when you were at your lowest ebb and how each person reacted to you. Were they compassionate? Did they say just the right thing when you were at your most vulnerable? Did they offer help or support? Did they show you kindness? This is very important as it will show you who you truly need in your life and who enhances it. Take an honest look at those around you. Do you need these people? Are these people worth investing your precious time and energy in?

So now you must put in the steps to begin to attract more positive friends or family members into your life. You can do this by becoming the sort of friend that other people feel attracted to and want to have in their lives. Life is so very short, and you deserve the space to invite good people into your life.

Relationship De-Clutter Affirmations

'I say goodbye to (name of person you wish to be free of) and wish them well with their own lives.'
'I give myself permission to cut people out of my life.'
'I deserve to attract good people into my life.'
'Life brings new opportunities to meet good friends.'
'I now have space to allow positive people into my life.'

Kindness

'Being kind to others will always reward you with gift of a good feeling towards yourself.'

The key concept here is "Kindness" when investing in others. Just like in the previous chapter, where we discussed the concept of applying kindness to yourself, it is vital within the REMIND approach to apply this to others too. When describing the concept of kindness towards other people, I teach my own clients the above mantra.

A good way of investing in other people is via random acts of kindness (RAK). A random act of kindness is basically doing something nice for another person without the expectation of getting anything back from them in return (you are not being exploited here). It is Anne Herbert who is frequently credited with starting the random acts of kindness movement after she had written a kind quotation on the back of a placemat in a restaurant in California in 1982.

Since then, there has been a global trend in spreading kindness to others and much research into the benefits of it too, leading to the establishment of the Random Acts of Kindness Foundation. Their aim is to spread kindness throughout communities including home, work, school etc.

It is crucial to invest in other people if you want to establish a more positive mindset and to allow the opportunity of worthy relationships to develop. To invest in others, it is important to demonstrate concern, kindness, and empathy. Connecting with others breaks down loneliness and isolation (Titmus, 2014, Withey, 2020). However, investing in others also means doing small acts of kindness which will benefit someone else. There is much anecdotal evidence which suggests that performing an act of kindness or showing concern for others can have a direct positive impact on mood. Almost as though the "giver" is the "receiver" of the kindness (Titmus, 2014, Withey, 2020).

It is crucial to maintain social contact either face to face or by other means virtually, such as Zoom, phone, Facebook, Messenger etc. You can also show concern by sending a physical handwritten card or letter. Small acts of kindness for others in your community, such as posting a note through a neighbour's door, offering to do shopping etc. Any small act of kindness which you invest in another person will directly impact on your own mental wellbeing.

What is interesting about kindness, is that unlike some other feelings like happiness or gratitude, kindness is mostly a behaviour (or action).

What is quite amazing is that when we perform a random act of kindness (especially for a stranger) it can rebound on us. So, performing an act of kindness for another person can trigger similar emotions of both gratitude and happiness in us.

Building in random acts of kindness into your daily routine (REMIND) by investing in others can significantly raise your mood and help you feel a connection to those around you. It can in short make you feel valued and needed, which triggers feelings of both gratitude and happiness.

Doing good for other people can also have wider benefits. For example, performing a random act of kindness can help trigger the production of oxytocin, which is frequently referred to as the "love hormone." An interesting effect of oxytocin is that it can help to lower blood pressure and instil a sense of optimism and hope. Kindness also helps to increase energy levels and strength, which can in turn help you to feel calmer. All these positive effects can then directly impact mood and can help improve depression.

Ten Kindness Activities to Make You Feel Great

1) If you see an elderly person who appears lonely, smile, and say hello (you might be the first person who has taken any notice of them in days or weeks)

2) If you are travelling on public transport and you see someone who needs a seat, offer up yours.

3) Offer to buy a coffee or lunch for the next homeless person you see on the street. Spend some time talking to them (that act, and conversation may prove to be life changing for them)

4) Make it your aim to smile and say hello to your neighbours (even if you have never done so before). You would be surprised to learn that many people do not know or take an interest in the people we live directly amongst.

5) In work, offer to make a co-worker a hot drink. Compliment them on their appearance.

6) Send an email to a co-worker to say how much you value them or appreciate their skills. Work is one of the biggest sources of stress and worry for people so being kinder and taking an interest in those you work with will reap many positive benefits.

7) If you are waiting in the queue of the shop and you see someone who appears anxious, stressed, worried etc. (or maybe they even just have less items than you), then offer up your place ahead of them. The gratitude they express to you will rebound and those around you will witness an act of kindness that can often appear contagious.

8) Most of us have far too many items in our homes and could benefit from decluttering. Give unwanted items to charity rather than holding on to them with the view of selling them at a later date. Give freely to others.

9) Offer to bake a cake, cook a meal, do some shopping to anyone who may be housebound/ ill etc.

10) If you have children, teach them how to be kind to others. Get them to play with other children who are lonely or new to the school. Teach children how to compliment others not to criticise. Kindness to others can start at any age but the sooner you start, the better it will be.

Invest in Others After Trauma

So, you know how to apply kindness to others? However, there may still be occasions when others do something so bad to you, that you simply cannot "move" past it. The event, actions, words, or deeds of others can remain for a lifetime. Simply put, we become traumatised and end up in a spiral of replaying what was said, done or happened, repeatedly.

Holding grudges is self-destructive, negative and keeps you feeling trapped. In essence, holding onto grudges gives away your power to the perpetrator. Yet forgiveness can help you to reclaim your power and set you free.

Have you ever noticed how some people seem to turn the most seemingly dreadful event into a positive, by using it to turn their lives around? This process is known as posttraumatic growth (PTG).

The term was first developed in the mid-1990s by two psychologists called Richard Tedeschi and Lawrence Calhoun. It is based around the fact that people who have experienced psychological difficulties following traumatic events or adversities can develop a positive outlook and personal growth after. The authors developed five key areas in which people can use an adverse experience: **Personal Strength, New Possibilities, Relating to Others, Appreciation of Life and Spiritual Change** (Tedeschi & Calhoun, 1996). Forgiveness is therefore a key aspect of the REMIND approach and in investing in both self and others.

From the early pioneering work by Dr Tedeschi and Dr Calhoun, PTG is now widely accepted as being one of the major ways of transforming your life following an adverse experience/s. This happens when you can make sense of the trauma and view it in a different way to experience a life transformation in one or more of the established five key areas (Tedeschi et al, 2017).

You can use the trauma as a basis to turn the negative event into something positive. Examples of this can be people who have experienced serious childhood abuse who then (as adults) spend their lives helping other survivors. Another example can be recovering addicts (i.e., drug, alcohol, gambling etc.) who then help other people struggling with addictions. People who have been bereaved often become bereavement counsellors themselves and this is another example of PTG in action. In fact, the list and the opportunities for posttraumatic growth are seemingly endless. It is about becoming more aware of the potentially positive impact that a negative experience can have.

Take a moment to consider what it is that really affects you? Consider how the event has impacted upon you? Try to look and see whether there are any positive aspects to your life or yourself which have resulted because of this trauma.

One of the common features of PTG is that people frequently develop a greater empathy and understanding of others who have been in a similar situation to themselves.

Many are able put more effort and appreciation into their current relationships following an adverse event, so you develop a greater appreciation for the people you already have in your life. This is often a common feature I have observed in people who have faced serious life-changing illnesses, such as cancer. Having a potentially terminal illness can make people re-evaluate the good that exists in those, around them (such as family, friends, neighbours etc.) more. However, you do not need to have to face the potential of a serious illness to do so. Begin now by thinking consciously of all those people you currently have in your life who matter most to you.

So, using a negative experience can be a good way of investing in others to enhance posttraumatic growth. Forgiveness is a key part of the REMIND approach in investing in others so that you can lead a more fulfilled life.

Forgiveness

'Forgiveness will set you free.'

I use the above mantra to explain the complex purpose of forgiveness to the people I work with. In investing in others, it is also important to forgive those who may have harmed us too. You do not have to like or even have anything whatsoever to do with them, but forgiveness is key. Forgiving another person who has harmed you in any way does not mean you are "approving" of what they have done but it is a crucial way of freeing yourself from the damaging and toxic hold that keeps you connected to them.

Forgiveness is about you, not the other person. You are placing your own self-worth and self-love above that of the other person. You are re-claiming your power, by refusing to allow the event or actions of those who have harmed you to no longer have a hold over you.

Professor Loren Toussaint, from Luther College in Iowa, has spent several years researching the impact of forgiveness on our heath. He believes that almost everyone can benefit psychologically from being more forgiving. Toussaint and his colleagues published work in 2016, which investigated the role that forgiveness plays in both mental and physical health in young adults. They found that adopting a more forgiving attitude towards others can significantly help to reduce stress-related disorders. Forgiveness can really be a boost towards both mental and physical health (Toussaint et al, 2016).

In their book, *Live Happy*, Bridget Grenville-Cleave and Ilona Boniwell, report how forgiveness can help to lower blood pressure and plays a part in recovery from cardiovascular, stress related problems (Grenville-Cleave and Boniwell, 2019).

Forgiveness is good for us, but holding onto grudges is bad for our mind, body, and spiritual health. However, forgiveness is something that needs to be worked at as many people can struggle with the concept of forgiving another who has harmed them. Professor Toussaint believes that many people feel they are not capable of forgiving. However, this is not the case. He urges people to keep on trying to forgive, even if you struggle with the concept. He uses the example of dieting and then having cake during the diet. Having the occasional cake is a setback on your journey to losing weight. Just like forgiveness, you may have setbacks where you feel you cannot do it but keep trying and eventually you will find it becomes easier.

Also, it is important to forgive not just others who have harmed us but also ourselves. Be kind to yourself and forgive yourself. In investing in others, it is equally important to invest in forgiving yourself also.

Case Study

Tonia

Tonia is a 52-year-old married nurse with two grown up daughters. Tonia had been adopted into a loving family as a baby and was raised alongside her younger adopted sister. Both sisters had been adopted by a loving older couple who were unable to biologically have children.

Tonia described her childhood as "idyllic." However, neither she, not her sister knew they were adopted. When she was 18 her parents told her about the adoption, alongside her adopted sister. This had obviously been a shock for both girls, but they eventually came to terms with it.

Following the death of their parents Tonia and her adopted sister both decided that they wanted to trace their respective birth families. They contacted a local social worker who obtained the girls` original adoption files.

Tonia's sister managed to trace both her birth mother and birth father. She was welcomed into both of their respective families and found that she had a large extended birth family with several half siblings. It was an extremely happy outcome.

However, Tonia's experience was very different. Her birth mother had been a young unmarried 16-year-old girl at the time of her birth. She had been in care with no family. She had later been killed in a road accident aged only 20. It was devastating news for Tonia. No father was named on her adoption file, so she decided to take a commercially available DNA test in the hope of tracing some birth family.

After several months she was able to connect with a first cousin of her mother, who had no idea her mother had been born, let alone Tonia. The cousin was able to fill in parts of her family "story", but it was clear that Tonia was considered an "outsider" and eventually contact ceased.

She continued to check on her DNA test results. After a bit of "research" she was able to establish who her birth father had been. Sadly, he too was deceased. He had been a married man at the time of Tonia's birth who had two children (her half-sisters).

Both sisters refused to acknowledge Tonia as they viewed her as "evidence" of the betrayal of their mother by their father. This was devastating for Tonia. She faced a total "wall of silence." Not only had she discovered that both of her birth parents had died but her sisters had rejected her. This was a double blow as her adopted sister had found a loving, welcoming birth family who had accepted her unconditionally.

Tonia became very depressed. However, one of the major things she was struggling with was the anger and frustration that she felt towards her birth family and her adoptive parents for preventing her from searching for her birth family. She felt that if she had been able to find her father when he was still alive when she was younger, then maybe he and her sisters would have welcomed her. She felt she had left it "too late" in life.

Forgiveness was introduced as a way of moving forward. Being able to forgive her adoptive parents for not allowing her to search was important as she was then able to take a more compassionate view. Her adoptive parents clearly loved both Tonia and her sister very much and were fearful that if they had found their birth families, then they would no longer be "needed" and would leave them. By taking a more compassionate approach towards their situation she was not only able to forgive her adoptive parents but also to express gratitude for them "choosing" her as a baby and for them giving her a very happy and secure childhood.

Tonia found it slightly harder to forgive her birth sisters at first. Tonia's first instinct at finding out she had two sisters had been sheer delight and joy. She naturally wanted to meet them. However, their reaction to her appearance (even after the initial shock had waned) was still painful. Eventually, Tonia was able to take a fresh look at the situation by having compassion for the people who had rejected her. So rather than being angry towards them she was able to turn her frustration to compassion. In doing so, she was then able to forgive them for rejecting her.

In terms of posttraumatic growth, Tonia feels a greater sense of empathy towards other people who have been adopted and have been rejected by their birth families. She can take a more compassionate view of her own situation and to forgive those who have hurt her. In doing so, Tonia has freed herself of the emotional pain and the need to have these "biological strangers" (her words) in her life. She was also more able to express gratitude for all the loving people in her life including her husband and her daughters. Her adopted sister also made sure that Tonia was fully included as her "true" sister into her own new family and now has a wonderful, extended blended family.

Tonia's case is an example of how forgiveness can be both liberating and can lead to posttraumatic growth in a positive way.

Forgiveness Affirmations.
'I forgive (name) because I deserve to be set free.'
'I send (name) away with forgiveness and light.'
'Forgiving others sets me free of the past.'
'I release (name) from hurting me.'
'I forgive myself.'
'I deserve the right to forgive others.'

Summary

So, we have considered the "I" in terms of investing in both self and others and how it is a vital component in the REMIND approach. Investing in self helps us to develop our own sense of worth and place in the world, together with how our actions impact on those around us too. By investing in ourselves we can learn what our unique strengths and limitations are, which in turn can lead to discovering your true vocation in life. Investing in other people, has the added benefit of improving our own wellbeing and in improving our social and emotional interaction with others. Investing in others is good for the mind and soul. Therefore, the I in the REMIND approach is inextricably linked to investing in self and other people too. No man (or woman) is an "island."

Chapter 6
N = Nature

'Our task must be to widen our circle of compassion to embrace all living creatures and the whole of nature in its beauty.'
(Albert Einstein)

The Link Between Nature and Wellbeing

The "N" in the REMIND approach stands for nature. The importance of being within nature cannot be over stressed in terms of mental and physical health. The UK charity Mind (2018) encourages people to try to be exposed to nature and natural settings as much as possible as they have proven effects on both mental and physical wellbeing. Obviously, being outside will also encourage the natural production of vitamin D, which is linked to a healthy immune system too (vital at this time) (Grenville-Cleave and Boniwell, 2019).

The Mental Health Foundation suggests that nature is a critical part of maintaining good mental health. They offer several definitions in terms of what "nature" is. These include green spaces such as woodlands, forests, and parks. They can also include "blue spaces" such as beaches, rivers, canals, and wetlands. However, if you live in an urban area, nature can be found on streets, such as trees, plants, bushes, grass verges, window boxes and potted plants. Therefore, no matter where you live, there is always the potential to access nature.

Even watching nature documentaries or television programs that incorporate nature has a beneficial impact upon mental wellbeing (Mental Health Foundation, 2021).

It was during the Pandemic that the importance of nature really became of pressing importance. In the UK alone nearly half of the population (45%) reported that visiting green spaces enabled them to cope psychologically in an uncertain and ever-changing world (The Mental Health Foundation, 2021).

A study was conducted by Mathew White, and colleagues based at the European Centre for Environment and Human Health at the University of Exeter, investigating the amount of time spent in nature. What they found was very interesting in terms of both physical and mental wellbeing. Their work involved almost 20,000 people and demonstrated that spending just 120 minutes a week in natural settings such as parks or other green spaces, significantly influenced both mental and physical health. What was also interesting was the fact that it could be spread across the week, so for example, one long period and several shorter ones. The important factor was the amount of time and the fact that it needed to be a minimum of 120 minutes (just two hours) a week (White et al., 2019).

Therefore, I encourage my own clients to engage with concepts of nature as much as possible. Using the REMIND approach to structure your day, so that you build in aspects of nature. There are lots of different ways in which you can incorporate the natural world into your everyday routine. The obvious one is to take regular exercise outside, amongst green space. However, the following suggestions will also demonstrate how to do so in other purposeful and meaningful activities.

The Power of Gardening

Lack of access to available green spaces does not necessarily mean an inability to connect with nature as suggested by the Mental Health Foundation. Consider aspects of nature that you can access rather than what you cannot. If you have a garden, then this is just as effective. It is the process of being outside and being mindful to the environment. If you do not have a garden, do you have a window? Sitting by an open window and feeling the rays of sunlight, the coolness of the breeze, the external sounds can be very positive.

Gardening is extremely beneficial and impacts greatly upon mental health (Mind, 2018). Again, plants can be grown from seed in containers on a windowsill if you do not have a garden. The process of nurturing a living plant and watching it grow, not only helps with mood but also feeds into achievement and instils a sense of hope and optimism in the future.

Gardening and connecting with the soil help to promote a sense of being connected to one`s immediate environment. Almost as though you are instilling a sense of being part of something much "bigger" than yourself. We are all part of the world around us (no matter how much you may think that you are not) and gardening helps to instil that sense.

During the Global Pandemic there was an exponential rise in people taking up and growing plants or vegetables for the first time. The need to connect with nature during long periods of isolation and Lockdown was evident. The natural instinct of being amongst nature proved to be a primal driving force for many people.

An important component of gardening is being outside. Not just outside in the sunshine but in all weathers and seasons too.

Gardening helps people to stay physically fit in addition to contributing to overall mental health. It helps to lower blood pressure and ignite a sense of both optimism and hope, together with providing meaning and purposeful activity. So, what are you waiting for? Even if you live in a high-rise apartment in the city. Open a window, buy some seeds, compost, and containers, and start to connect with nature.

Mindfulness in Nature

Immerse yourself fully in any aspect of the natural world. One of my favourite things is to listen in a focused way to morning birdsong. Even if you live in a city. If you concentrate and listen with your full attention you can become aware to the sounds of nature around, you (even amongst traffic noise).

Whilst walking outside, pay attention to how your body feels as you walk amongst nature. Feel the breeze on your face, the wind in your hair (or upon your skin if you are bald!). Walk in all weathers and seasons. Never save walking or being outside to just fine weather. In doing so, you are missing all the aspects of being fully connected. Feel the rain on your face, the cool air, the hailstones, and snow. You can always dress appropriately for any weather and get out to enjoy all that the seasons of the year must gift you. I use the term "gift" as being outside is a gift. Nature is an ever-changing gift which has lots of wonderful aspects to deliver to us. It is there for our taking, so we just need to notice and pay attention to it.

Engage more in the sensory aspects of nature fully. The different smells and sights of the seasons are a favourite of mine. In the autumn the leaves change in the most spectacular of ways and deliver their true hidden colours. As they fall, mindfully engage in trying to catch a leaf. You may have done this as a child but the wonder of catching a falling leaf in autumn is an amazing gift to all of us. Notice the smells in the air during autumn that you will not find at any other time.

You can do this for all the seasons of the year from autumn, winter, spring, and summer. All of them are different and unique and offer ways to develop a greater sense of connectivity to nature.

How lovely is it to feel the sun on your skin again during the summer? Or maybe when you see the first daffodil appearing on a grass verge you have the optimism of spring and new life emerging? Each season is a unique sensory experience which allows us to be fully present in the moment and to be mindful of our place in the world.

Animals and Nature

"We are all part of the natural world"

Anyone who owns a pet will tell you how caring for an animal significantly helps with their mental wellbeing. Owning a pet is another wonderful way of connecting to nature. Humans may think they have "supreme power" on this planet, but we are the minority species.

Research has found that animals (particularly dogs) can really help with both our physical and mental health. Again, it was noticeable that during the Pandemic pet ownership rose as we sought ways to connect with the natural world around us. Walking a dog gives us purpose and meaning. It allows us to connect with the world around us whilst giving us valuable exercise in all seasons and in all weathers. Dog walking is also an extremely valuable way of helping us to feel more sociable too. For example, people who regularly walk their dogs are far more likely to feel a connectivity and sense of community amongst those who also walk their pets.

However, it is not just dogs. Cats are also a source of connecting with nature even if we cannot take them for a walk! Stroking our pets helps to lower blood pressure and is an excellent way of reducing stress and keeping mindfully in the present.

Caring for another creature helps to provide a sense of meaning and purpose which in turn acts as a boost to our self-efficacy (what we can do well) and our self-esteem.

Overall pet and animal ownership really helps us to connect more fully with nature, boosting physical and mental wellbeing.

13 Activities to Connect with Nature

1) Grow plants outside or indoors.
2) Walking outside in all weathers and all seasons.
3) Pay careful attention to the sights, smells, sounds and sensations of nature around you.
4) Exercise (particularly cycling and running) outside.
5) Visit a park.
6) Visit a beach.
7) Visit remote places where you have never been before.
8) Take a picnic and sit and enjoy it mindfully in an outside place (even your garden is enough).
9) Smell the flowers. As you walk, notice any flowers or plants around you. One of my favourite things to do (which I have done ever since I was a small child) is to smell roses which may overhang into the street where you walk. I love to smell the scent of flowers. You can do this for any plant or even vegetables. Sniff them and fully take in the scent of nature.
10) Walk amongst trees. Find a tree that you like. Sit down with your back against the trunk. Close your eyes and mindfully become aware of the feel of the bark against your back, the roots beneath you

going deep into the earth. Listen to the sound of leaves blowing gently in the breeze. Pay attention to the sounds of nature around you. You will find that this exercise really helps to relax and centre you, whilst being amongst nature. Trees are an excellent resource most of us can find, whether we live in rural or urban areas (i.e., public parks/ greenspaces).

11) Pick flowers or plants and fully focus all your attention on their shape, colour, scent, and textures. Again, another favourite childhood activity of mine, is to pick dandelion "clocks" and to blow their seeds into the wind. In reconnecting with the childlike self, you also connect with nature.

12) Cold water swimming or "wild swimming." There is a growing trend in the UK for wild swimming in cooler water all year round. This can be in the sea, in rivers or lakes etc. There are lots of groups and societies which you can join which promote this within natural settings. Do your research, find one and try it. Cold water swimming has lots of mental and physical health benefits and is an excellent way of connecting to nature.

13) Practice meditation amongst nature. People who regularly meditate outside find that it helps them to focus in a more positive way on the world around them and their connectedness to it.

Nature Affirmations.
'Nature feeds my mind, body and soul.'

'I enjoy being outside.'

'The sounds of nature fill me with happiness (hope, contentment etc.).'

'All weather brings new gifts and experiences.'

'Feeling the rain, wind, sun etc. fills me with life.'

'I am part of nature and nature is part of me.'

Case Study

Tom.

Nature can have an enduring impact throughout our lives, even when we are at our most vulnerable or when we may not be able to convey our needs.

After suffering a series of strokes, Tom had lost his ability to speak and had become physically disabled. Unable to care for himself any longer he was admitted to a nursing home.

Whilst there, Tom spent almost all his time indoors and rarely ventured outside. The nursing staff and his family noticed that Tom had become extremely depressed and naturally assumed it was because he was dealing with the transition from his home to living in the nursing home. However, that was only part of it.

Tom had spent his whole working life as a gardener. After retiring he had spent his days tending to his own garden which he dearly loved. So, in addition to dealing to the loss of his independence, communication and home, Tom was grieving for the loss of his connection with nature too. His life had been spent outdoors, in all weathers and in all seasons amongst nature.

Tom needed to experience nature by being outside every day in his wheelchair. It was scheduled into his routine. It did not matter what the weather was like (he was always dressed appropriately). It was the exposure to the outside world. The nursing home was surrounded by a beautiful garden, so it was easy to achieve.

This simple adjustment to Tom's routine had a significant impact in raising his mood and helping him to reconnect with nature. The nursing home's gardener also got to know Tom and took him out regularly with him in his wheelchair whilst he was doing his duties, talking through the plants with Tom.

Nature can impact all of us no matter how old we are or even if we can no longer communicate our needs. Nature helps.

Summary

There are numerous reasons why nature is so vital to staying both mentally and physically well. Therefore, you should aim to include exposure to nature daily and for an absolute minimum of 120 minutes over the week. Incorporate nature into your daily routine and follow it with the REMIND approach. Remember "green is good"!

Chapter 7
D = Diet

'When diet is wrong, medicine is of no use. When diet is correct, medicine is of no need.'
(Ayurvedic Proverb)

The "D" in the REMIND approach stands for "Diet." The food we eat, and how we consume it plays a complex, yet significant part in how we feel. Food can both boost how you feel and literally "feed" into your own sense of wellbeing. Yet, other foods can worsen stress and anxiety, making you feel a whole lot worse.

As a therapist, I see every day how food impacts on a person`s social and emotional wellbeing. A regular healthy diet with set mealtimes (including not skipping breakfast) should be part of your daily routine (Telloian, 2019). A diet rich in nutrients will not only make you feel better physically and mentally but it will also contribute to a healthy immune system.

Comfort eating large quantities of junk, fatty foods is certainly not uncommon in people with either anxiety or depression. It can become a spiral. The initial sensation of eating something sweet or fatty can temporarily lead to feeling "good" but the more you consume the less "good" you feel about yourself. It is often accompanied by feelings of guilt, disgust or even self-loathing. You may also gain weight, then think, "What the heck, I am fat now, so I might as well just eat whatever I want." Being fat or obese then brings all the associated feelings of low self-esteem, a lack of worth (not to mention the health complications of type two diabetes. Comfort eating just seems to spiral downwards so that you feel worse and worse about yourself.

At its extreme, eating disorders like anorexia or bulimia nervosa can ensue. Both are indications of control in negative ways and both link into complex mental health and self-esteem issues.

Therefore, diet in the REMIND approach is a vital component to live well and aid mental and physical wellbeing.

Foods to Improve Mood: Mental Health and Diet

'Let food be thy medicine, thy medicine shall be thy food.'
(Hippocrates – Ancient Greek Philosopher)

What is known about mood and diet is that certain vitamins, minerals and food groups have a definitive impact on raising mood.

The authors Grenville-Cleave and Boniwell (2019) in their book, *Live Happy*, suggest eating a diet containing the following nutrients as these all impact mood positively: folic acid, vitamin B-12, vitamin C, selenium, iron and essential fatty acids like omega-3.

Foods that are rich in protein are also a crucial part in maintaining mental wellbeing. Amino acids are contained within protein. Amino acids help in the chemical process that regulates thoughts and feelings. Protein can be found in fish, eggs, peas, beans, nuts, seeds, and lean meat. Protein also has an additional benefit too. It keeps you feeling fuller for longer, so you are less likely to either snack on biscuits, crisps etc. or get trapped in the cycle of comfort eating. Tryptophan is an extremely important amino acid that helps in the production of the "feel good" chemical serotonin. Serotonin is important in helping you to feel calm and better about yourself. It can be found in bananas, oats, milk, cheese, nuts, turkey, and chicken.

Healthy fats (fatty acids) are an essential part of staying mentally well. The brain needs healthy fats such as omega three and six so that it can work at its best. Omega-3 is a long chain fatty acid that really helps in combatting stress. Like foods rich in tryptophan, omega-3 helps to boost serotonin production in the brain. Emerging research also indicates that it may help in reducing the risk of heart disease. Healthy fats can be found in oily fish such as salmon, tuna, sardines, and herring. They can also be found in shellfish, avocado, tofu, nuts and seeds (including walnuts, almonds, sunflower, pumpkin chia and flaxseeds), poultry, olive and sunflower oils, milk, yogurt (particularly live and Greek), eggs and cheese.

Vitamin B is vital in mood regulation. For example, folic acid and vitamin B-12 are particularly effective in helping to boost mood and a deficiency in both can sometimes trigger depression. Good sources of vitamin B include red meat Such as beef and pork), chicken, eggs, dark green leafy vegetables citrus fruits, nuts, and rice.

Complex carbohydrates also help the brain to produce serotonin. Good sources of complex carbohydrates can be found in whole-wheat bread and pasta, sweet potatoes, bananas, beans, peas, and brown rice.

Fluid intake is also vital to mental wellbeing and to avoid becoming dehydrated. The brain is highly composed of water, so if you become dehydrated you will find that you have difficulty concentrating, experience headaches and experience changes to your mood. Dehydration also leads to constipation (which several of my own patients with depression frequently report). Therefore, it is vital to maintain good hydration. It is recommended that you drink between 6–8 glasses of fluid a day. I prefer water, but it can also be made up of tea, herbal teas, coffee, juice etc. However, be mindful of the amount of both caffeine and sugar you take in which is the advice provided by the charity Mind in 2021. In general, avoid diet drinks which contain artificial sweeteners as these are not good for your overall health.

Mediterranean Diet

There is much evidence that following a Mediterranean diet can really help in terms of both physical and mental health. An in-depth review was conducted by a team of Italian academics in 2020 which demonstrated how the Mediterranean diet is proving to be really promising in helping people to really feel fit and healthy (Ventriglio et al, 2020). The Mediterranean diet consists of fruit, vegetables, pulses, nuts, white meat, fish, and olive oil. Moderate to low amounts of fermented dairy products and red meats are also included. Interestingly, it also advocates for a low intake of red or white wine during the main meal. However, if you do decide to follow this way of eating, do follow the guidance in terms of alcohol consumption (especially if you have problems with addiction).

Alcohol

Alcohol is something that many people with mood disorders struggle with. Although moderate alcohol consumption (particularly one small of glass of red wine a day which has some benefits) is the recommended limit. Large quantities of alcohol are extremely damaging in terms of both physical and mental health. If you cannot stop at the limit of one small glass of red wine a day (and lots of people cannot, particularly those with addiction issues) then avoid alcohol. This may seem like straightforward advice, but the reality is that alcohol consumption can make your depression worse (Withey, 2020).

However, if you do not struggle with addiction and you want to enjoy the occasional drink, then do so mindfully. Make sure you pour your favourite drink into the finest glassware you have. Do not drink it whilst doing other activities. You need to savour it. Sip it slowly and really notice the taste, temperature, and smell of it. Feel how the glass you sip from feels against your lip. Really enjoy it and sip only small mouthfuls. Do this very slowly. Have a glass of water at the same time and take sips between your alcoholic drink. This will fill you up so that you do not become too thirsty, in addition to acting as a "palate cleanser" so that your mouth can fully savour the unique taste and sensation of the alcohol – rather than becoming accustomed to it. In this way you will fully enjoy your occasional treat and you will not overindulge. In other words, enjoy your drink and do so mindfully.

Look After Your Gut

The Mental Health Foundation in 2021 published information about how diet impacts on mental wellbeing. For example, they highlight the link between gut health and mental health. This is also raised by the mental health charity Mind (2021). If a person is feeling anxious or depressed it can directly impact digestion making the gut either speed up or slow down. In addition to avoiding stress and improving mood, the gut needs to aid healthy digestion by having foods rich in fibre and fluid combined with regular exercise (the "E" in the REMIND approach).

Gut "friendly" foods include vegetables, whole grains, pulses, beans, fruits, and probiotics such as live yogurts. Try to eat a range of different coloured fruit and vegetables each day as these contain a range of vitamins, minerals, and nutrients we need in order to stay mentally well.

It is vital in addition to eating healthily, to learn how to manage your stress levels as the stress response has a direct impact on digestion and your gut.

Foods to Eat Less of

The occasional treat should be just that, "occasional." For example, some carbohydrates like chocolates, biscuits, white bread etc., can help in the production of mood boosting serotonin. It is one of the reasons why you feel "good" immediately after eating them. However, these effects are extremely short lived as they are soon followed by a drop in blood sugar levels that end up making you feel lethargic or even depressed (not to mention associated weight gain).

So, in order to invest in yourself and your diet try to eat less of, or avoid, foods that are going to make you feel worse and are not healthy including: Cakes, pastries, biscuits, refined sugar, processed/ ready meals, sausages, pies, pasties, food fried in hydrogenated fat (like chips, burgers, fried chicken, fast food). Try to limit your amount of salt (sodium) intake too.

However, if you are eating nutritious food most of the time, give yourself the permission to indulge in the occasional treat. Do not feel guilty for the odd blip here and there. We are all human. If you are mostly aiming to eat nutritious foods and you feel good, then having an occasional cake is no big deal. If you do have a treat, then do so mindfully so that you fully enjoy it and savour every mouthful. Eat it slowly and enjoy the taste. Give your treat your full attention. Try to avoid eating anything quickly or whilst doing something else at the same time (mindlessly). Treats are to be both savoured and enjoyed, so if you do give in to the chocolate, make sure to "give in" in a mindful way. You will find that you enjoy it more, you will consume less, and you will not feel guilty.

Learn to Cook

Sadly, many people have never learnt how to cook nutritious meals from scratch. In fact, many pupils at school do not learn the basics and if they are brought up in homes where there is a reliance on convenience foods, it is unlikely that these skills have been passed on. Over the years, I have seen an increasing number of young people who have never been taught the basics of cooking meals from scratch.

Also, many adults have simply lost the ability due to a reliance on food that is quick but lacks the nutrients.

Therefore, it is vital to not only apply the REMIND approach – "D" in diet but also the "I" in terms of invest in self and others, to acquire the skill of cooking. Invest in yourself by learning this skill. You can take online classes in addition to in person classes. Watch cookery programs (there are a plethora on television). Buy a cookery book and follow simple recipes.

Overall, if you cannot cook, invest in yourself by learning to do so. It will lead to a new skill set that will benefit you psychologically, physically, and financially too.

Get Organised and Plan Ahead

To stick to a healthy balanced diet, it is vital to plan your meals ahead (particularly if you are cooking for a family). Take a shopping list with you with the ingredients you need for each meal. That way you will stay on track and avoid the temptation of buying unnecessary goods or items which are on "offer." Cooking meals from scratch is also more economic than purchasing convenience or "ready meals", and more nutritious too. Follow closely simple recipes.

Cook meals in advance. People who tend to "stay on track" with their diets or healthy eating do so because they can access food easily. Try to get into the habit of cooking batches of meals in advance and then freeze them. So, cook more than you need at the time and freeze the excess. In doing so, you will always have a healthy and nutritious home cooked meal that you can simply pop into the microwave or oven on the days when you are either struggling for time or when you are having a "bad" day.

How to Dine Like Royalty

You do not need to be a king or queen to dine like you are the most important person in the world. However, you need to treat yourself as though you are, no matter what you are eating. This is a constant concept I use in therapy.

Always use your finest crockery, cutlery, and glassware. Even if you are eating simple porridge, beans on toast or just drinking water. It does not matter. It is the ritual of dining and making it feel as though it is an occasion which is crucial.

Eight-step Plan

This 8-step set routine is one which I follow myself for everyday meals at home. This ritual can be used whether you live alone or with other people. If you are a family, I always suggest set evening mealtimes so that you can turn family meals to social occasions too:

1) **Always eat at a table.** If you do not have a table, use a substitute. For example, a coffee, table, desk, an upturned box (anything as long as it can be used as a table, so you are not balancing your meal on your lap). Sitting in an upright position also helps you to digest food better.

2) **Set the table.** Lay your condiments and cutlery out ahead of your meal. Place a tablecloth on, placemats etc. Make your table look as beautiful as you can.

3) **Light a candle.** If you have a candle (especially for evening meals) then light it whilst you are dining. It helps to make your meal feel special like it is an occasion.

4) **Turn off any social media, televisions, or radios etc.** You need to give the meal your full attention. Never, ever multitask or have external stimuli on whilst eating.

5) **Use the finest crockery you have.** Use it daily and never save things for "best." You will notice that charity shops are filled with people's finest glasses and crockery which have seen very little use in their lifetimes. Most people have items in their cupboards that they feel are not "worth" using on a daily basis as they are too "good." Just think of all those charity shop items or those in antique shops that came from people's homes that they were "saving for best" and now it is too late! Use them now. Not in the future. You are worthy.

6) **Finest glassware.** If you drink water with your meal, then pour it into a beautiful wine glass or champagne flute. You will notice how much more you will enjoy it!

7) **Pay careful attention to the presentation of the food on your plate.** We tend to eat with our "eyes" so we are more likely to enjoy our meals if they are presented well. I tend to eat yogurt for breakfast. So instead of eating it from the plastic tub it comes from, I place it into a glass and eat it mindfully using a teaspoon.

8) **Eat slowly and mindfully at all times.** Chew your food slowly. Taste your food and focus your attention fully on the taste, sensation, and texture as you chew, suck, sip each mouthful. Savour the taste of your food and really notice it. As you swallow pay attention to how it feels as the food travels down to your stomach. Approach every mouthful of food in this way, focusing all your attention fully. Pay attention to the taste of all the different food stuffs on your plate. As you progress through your meal, pay attention to how satisfied you feel. When you feel full, stop eating. Eating mindfully like this will allow you to become more in tune to how your body feels whilst eating and gives you an indication of how much food you actually need. Mindful eating prevents you from overeating (comfort eating) too. You will find that if you eat mindfully, you will enjoy whatever you eat more fully.

Social Eating

As humans we are innately social beings. Our primitive ancestors ate together in their caves around a fire. Social dining is part of our DNA and the reason why we enjoy dining out so much in restaurants. So, if you are fortunate enough to be treated to an occasional restaurant or café meal, do not spend the time on your phone. Engage fully with whoever you are with at the time.

The Mental Health Foundation (2021) suggest that there are lots of social, psychological, and biological benefits to be gained by sharing meals with other people. They help to promote a sense of routine and "rhythm" to our lives which feeds into a sense of purpose and meaning. From a physiological perspective, dining whilst sat upright helps to aid digestion, whilst talking to other people and listening to others during conversation, helps to slow eating down (Mental Health Foundation, 2021).

During the Pandemic, dining out with friends or family became an almost impossible task. It remains an almost impossible task for many people who live away from friends and family too. However, spending mealtimes with those we care for can still be achieved no matter if they live on the other side of the world. This is where social media and facilities like Zoom can really be used as tools to enhance connectedness with others during times of isolation or distance.

Set a mealtime and use Zoom (or whatever other social platform) to connect with friends and family. A good way of "sharing a meal" is to agree to cook the same recipe and to serve up the meal the same way. That way you can fully immerse yourselves in both the shared experience of food and the preparation of the meal. If you are in a group, take it in turns to come up with a recipe. Turn the experience into a weekly or monthly event so that you feel connected with others during times when you cannot meet face to face.

Apply all the same principles of mindful eating and dining to your social dining experiences, whether these are in virtual contexts or face to face.

Be Gentle on Yourself

Be kind to yourself and allow yourself the occasional "blip." It is normal when you are trying to establish any new habits to occasionally "fall off the wagon." The trick is to get back on that "wagon" as soon as you can. When trying to set new ways of eating and thinking about food it is a fact that you may succumb to your old ways from time to time. Be kind on yourself. You can always start again the next day. It is important to reward the effort you are making towards a new life and building diet into your REMIND approach.

Common Childhood Food Myths

Eating patterns are often established in childhood. Sadly, so is guilt, shame, and "rewards" around food.

It is not uncommon for parents to say things like the following to children:

'If you do not eat all of your dinner, then you will not have pudding.'

This instils the habit of eating beyond being full (overeating) and using food as a reward, so children learn to make the association between what they term "good" and "bad" foods. A treat is seen as "good." So, it is not unusual that later in life many adults feel like they must eat every morsel on their plates whether they are full or not. The savoury aspect of the meal then comes to be associated with food that must be "endured" rather than enjoyed. It is quite a complex pattern.

Another common phrase often used by parents in relation to food is:

'There are starving people in the world who would be grateful for your food.'

This phrase often instils a sense of guilt in children so, again, there is the feeling that you are "lucky" to have food, rather than you deserve food.

These are just two examples of common phrases used by parents almost everywhere. However, if you are brought up hearing statements like this as a child, then it is not surprising that so many adults have complex relationships with their diets.

Try not to feel guilty. You are human. You have had a lifetime of feeling guilty around food so make the effort to turn that guilt into compassion. Treat yourself always with kindness.

Diet Affirmations.

'I feed my body with nutritious food!'

'I am worthy of eating healthy food.'

'If I slip, I forgive myself.'

'I have come a long way on my journey.'

'I congratulate myself on making healthy choices.'

'I deserve nutritious food.'

'I enjoy my food.'

'I am focused on savouring every mouthful of every meal.'

'I enjoy the occasional treat.'

Summary

The D in the REMIND approach stands for diet. Diet is crucial in maintaining good mental health. How we present and eat our food is crucial in terms of a sense of wellbeing. So never save your best crockery for a "special occasion." Make every meal an "occasion." Foods that contain the following mood boosting properties are extremely important including amino acids like tryptophan, complex carbohydrates, protein, omega three and six fatty acids, vitamins B and C. A diet like the Mediterranean diet is a good starting point. Allow yourself the occasional treat and avoid feeling guilty. Aim to eat your food slowly and mindfully and enjoy the experience whilst doing so.

Chapter 8
REMIND Approach in Action

In summary, REMIND stands for:

R – Routine.
E – Exercise.
M – Mindfulness.
I – Invest in self and others.
N – Nature.
D – Diet.

So now it is about incorporating each of these components into your daily life to help you to live a life worth living and to find the happiness and fulfilment you need.

The REMIND approach offers a structure which can be used flexibly to fit around your individual needs in terms of life, work, family, friends, leisure etc. It can also be used to help set goals and to note your achievements along the way too.

In therapy it is very common to use diaries with patients and clients to help set patterns and to record progress and achievements. It is also to see what patterns and events are linked to certain behaviours or triggers. It can also be a way of reminding yourself how far you have come on your journey too.

What people tend to like is a structure that is simple to follow in establishing new patterns of behaviours. For this reason, I recommend my clients fill out a simple daily REMIND diary sheet, which you can find below. It can be used flexibility and is divided into morning, afternoon, and evening slots. You can also use it to record your thoughts alongside each component, together with the goals you wish to achieve. Remember to keep these goals SMART and start off small. That way, you are more likely to stay motivated and hopeful.

You can also record daily affirmations too on your form. In doing so you will be creating a more positive and expansive mindset. Writing down affirmations is a powerful way of reinforcing the meaning of the words to your brain and how they link into your daily life.

The important thing is to find a way that works for you and your unique life to incorporate each element of REMIND.

REMIND APPROACH DAILY DIARY
Please fill in each day.

Day Date	Morning	Afternoon	Evening
R Routine			
E Exercise			
M Mindfulness			
I Invest in self and others			
N Nature			
D Diet			

Case Study

Peter

Peter is a 35-year-old man who was experiencing difficulties during the National Covid Lockdown of 2020. Until the imposed Lockdown Peter had been working as a busy restaurant manager, but then found himself at home, living alone, no work life, limited social contact and feeling desperate. It was a time of great uncertainty and fear for many people, but for those living alone, like Peter, Covid really impacted upon both his mental and physical health.

A month before the Lockdown Peter had separated from his partner Bill of four years, ironically due to the unsocial hours he was keeping at work and the fact that they were subsequently leading separate lives. Peter and Bill had been very much in love before the split and no one else had been involved.

Peter felt, his life had been plunged into chaos. He was staying up into the early hours of the morning playing online games. He had difficulty sleeping and spent most of the following day in bed. He had started to drink quite heavily and was ordering online grocery shopping and supplies so that he did not need to leave his flat. He had lost his meaning, purpose, and direction in life.

He had gained a lot of weight and had totally stopped exercising. Prior to the Lockdown he had attended a local gym twice a week, in addition to being very active in his job. Now he was not exercising at all (even though the government had recommended an hour outside each day). Apart from the online gaming community he was not directly interacting with anyone. His partner Bill had attempted multiple times to contact Peter, but he was ignoring all his calls and messages as he just felt so depressed.

Here is how the REMIND approach was used to get Peter's life back on track:

Routine

It was essential to establish a healthy daily base line for Peter with regulated sleep. He used the four-step morning routine procedure. The sleep restriction method was included to help Peter to set his sleeping patterns and to establish restful sleep. He also needed to restrict the time he was spending online gaming. Peter was encouraged to invest in his physical appearance during his self-care routine.

Exercise

Peter had stopped all forms of exercise, so it was essential to find a way of building it into his daily routine. He began by incorporating dance into his morning routine as he was reluctant at first to venture outside. Once he had established his confidence and had seen the positive impact of moving through dance on his mood, he was more willing to venture out. He began by setting achievable goals of short daily walks. As Peter had gained weight, he felt self-conscious so wanted to limit as few people as possible "seeing him." He feared "bumping into" his previous partner Bill as he was ashamed of how he appeared. So initially the walks took place very early in the morning. As his confidence and fitness developed Peter then built up from shorts walks to longer ones (the full hour permitted outside at the time), then he began to build in jogging and eventually running. He began to lose weight which helped to raise both his mood and his self-confidence. Running became Peter's chosen daily exercise fitness routine as his physical fitness improved, which he really enjoyed. He varied his routes but always incorporated sections of his run through green spaces (his local park). Enjoyment was key to his motivation to continue.

Mindfulness

Peter learnt the essential component of living in the present moment, fully immersing himself in all he was doing, in a non-judgmental way. He was able to practice sensory mindfulness whilst running outside in all weathers, whilst doing his daily chores, preparing meals, eating and his other activities of self-care. He scheduled in mindful laughter by practicing the laughter exercises and by consciously seeking out humorous videos on the internet and television.

Invest in Self

This was a vital component here. He had to learn how to treat himself with both compassion and kindness. Up until Lockdown Peter had been investing all his attention to his job, but now it had gone. Therefore, he had to relearn the basics about gratitude and kindness for all that he had in life (including those around him). He discussed his job at length and how it had come at a cost to his relationships, social life and finding his true vocation. He had not been happy for a long time in his work but had not known just how this could be changed.

Peter completed the "My True Vocation" activity to find alternatives. One thing that emerged was how Peter had always wanted to become a journalist when he was both a child and as a young man. He had spent much of his childhood writing stories and later had taken an A` level in English Literature. He had decided not to go to university though as he feared getting into "debt." However, life had "got in the way" of his dreams and he had done a variety of different jobs, before drifting into his current position as a restaurant manager. Deep down he regretted the choices he had made and lacked fulfilment.

So, a vital part in investing in self is through learning. Peter did some research into online courses he could do at a distance during Lockdown and found a course in journalism which he signed up to. In doing so, he was putting his dreams into action and reclaiming control over his life, together with instilling hope. Peter's journalism course became a central part of his daily routine and a motivator for change. He also used visualisation as a way of staying positive and hopeful in the future.

Invest in Others

Peter had become lonely and isolated during Lockdown, which reinforced the importance of investing in others. He began by returning Bill's messages. Even though they had split up both had felt that this had been a mistake, so Peter began investing the love and attention in Bill that had been absent whilst focusing on his job. As they were now living separately, they could not meet up in person for a while due to the Lockdown restrictions, so they began a new "courtship" at a distance, which reignited their love for each other.

Peter also made the effort to contact his family (including his sister) and his wider circle of friends. Although meeting in person was impossible, it was a case of finding what they could do. So, Peter decided to arrange weekly quiz nights via Zoom where he invited friends and chosen family members to socialise, have fun and laugh together.

Prior to the Pandemic Peter had very little knowledge about his immediate neighbours. However, he knew there were several elderly people who lived alone in his street. So, Peter put a note through their doors introducing himself and telling them that he was available to collect shopping, prescriptions etc. or was free if they wanted a telephone call. This random act of kindness and investing in others significantly fed into Peter's own self-worth and really helped raise his mood, together with establishing stronger social links within his immediate community.

Nature

Peter's daily running routine made the most of incorporating green spaces via his local park. Becoming mindful of nature helped Peter to connect to aspects of the natural world during his runs, such as actively listening to the birds singing, dogs barking, the weather, the sound of the leaves in the wind, the scent of plants etc. All these aspects helped Peter feel more connected to his immediate surroundings and his place within nature.

Peter also took a keen interest in growing herbs in his kitchen, thus bringing aspects of the natural world into his home too.

Diet

Peter's diet had been a real area for concern at the start of his therapy. He was ordering ready meals in his weekly shopping delivery and eating a lot of chocolate, crisps, and cakes. This coupled with the alcohol which he was drinking whilst playing online games, had led to him gaining a lot of weight and a low sense of self. Although he did not consider his alcohol consumption a "problem" it was certainly an area he had to address.

Firstly, regular mealtimes were established. He used the "Dine Like Royalty" schedule so that he utilised his best crockery and glassware for each meal and sat at a table. As he re-built his relationship with Bill, they decided to eat their evening meal "together" via Zoom so that it was a social experience and an opportunity to reconnect with each other. This aspect worked well.

Peter also devoted more time to cooking meals from scratch using healthy ingredients. This was something he and Bill did together. They agreed to cook the same meal together over the internet at the same time in their respective kitchens. Not only were they sharing the experience of cooking but were eating the same food too. It fed into a sense of normality at a time when there was so much uncertainty.

Peter incorporated mindful eating so that he could savour his food. This helped to prevent him from snacking and bingeing on junk food, which had been part of his original problem.

In terms of alcohol consumption, Peter agreed not to drink alone. He limited his alcohol to one small glass each evening when he was dining with Bill. If for some reason Bill could not join him via Zoom, then he would not drink alcohol. However, what happened was that Peter stopped drinking altogether during the week, as he was so focused on his studies, his running, and his social life, he just did not feel the need!

Affirmations

Throughout, Peter selected daily affirmations which he would place in strategic areas around his home so he could easily see them and say them. They became an integrated part of his daily routine and helped him to establish gratitude, positivity, and hope in the future.

Peter – What Happened Next?

When Lockdown eventually lifted, Peter continued to incorporate REMIND into his daily life. He did not return to his previous job. He has recently completed his journalism studies and is now hopeful of a new, positive career. He and Bill are a couple and living together again. Peter is now leading a life worth living and fulfilling his potential. He is happier, healthier and more content than he has ever been. He now knows what both his strengths and limitations are and how he is directly connected to other people. Peter is a good example of how you too can use a REMIND approach to turn your life around and step into your power.

Case Study: Octavia

Octavia is a 47-year-old woman who was living with her 18-year-old daughter and their pet dog. Like in many recent cases, the isolation during Covid lockdown, had caused unresolved issues from the past to resurface resulting in a spiral into depression.

Prior to Lockdown, Octavia described her life as "existing." She was self-employed as a delivery driver, working long, unsociable hours. However, when the Covid Pandemic had struck, Octavia was too fearful of continuing her job and meeting people, so had ceased her work and hence her need to leave her home.

Following Lockdown, Octavia became significantly depressed and had lost her purpose and meaning in life. Her thoughts were dominated by her adverse childhood experiences, and she was suffering from intrusive flashbacks. She was not leaving her home. She was reliant on her daughter for shopping, cooking and for walking their dog.

She had previously taken great care in her physical appearance and had always "dyed her grey roots" and worn make up. However, since she was no longer able to face leaving her home, her self-care and appearance had also deteriorated.

Her daughter had resumed her college studies so was having to take on the added responsibility of caring for her mother too.

Her sleeping patterns were "chaotic." She frequently stayed up most of the night unable to rest watching television or on social media. During the day she spent most of it in lying in bed feeling fatigued, getting up when she felt able to. She had "lost interest" in food and had little appetite. Her daughter was doing most of the cooking, which meant they were both reliant on either "fast food" or "ready meals."

Her daughter had become increasingly worried about her mother, and it was she who had eventually persuaded her mother that she needed to seek help.

This is how the REMIND approach was used to help bring both purpose and meaning back into Octavia's life.

Routine

It was vital that Octavia was able to establish a daily routine which would instil hope, purpose and meaning. Keeping a daily diary helped her to see how she was using her time and where the areas of need were. She then used the four-step morning routine to build in a firm daily foundation. We used the sleep restriction method to help establish a more regular pattern of rest. It was also vital for Octavia that she realised early on that she was "worthy" of making the changes she needed to, to lead a more fulfilled life. So, affirmations were also key within her routine. Establishing a baseline routine of self-care was a crucial starting point here.

Exercise

As Octavia had got into the habit, during the Pandemic, of not leaving the house, she was engaged in very little physical exercise, which just exacerbated her fatigue/ energy levels. As her job had previously been a delivery driver, she had been used to being physically active dropping off parcels to people's homes and loading and unloading her van. She had always exercised by taking her dog out for long walks, both before and after work too. So, she was well "aware" of how little physical activity she was now engaging in.

Initially, she used the 30-second rule to help her break the cycle of fatigue and procrastination, incorporating the intense exercise of "on the spot" marching. This was also built into her daily routine for whenever she felt low in mood to provide an instant "boost."

Octavia grasped the concept of exercise being a mood enhancer, early on. A realistic form of exercise for her was to re-establish her early morning walks with her dog, starting with short walks (following her four-step morning routine). Her daughter was also extremely encouraging of her mother as she could see how her increased activity was impacting on her ability to do more. This acted as a big positive reinforcer and motivator for Octavia too.

As Octavia`s energy improved, her need to do more around the home also increased. She began taking on more household chores again, so that lessened the burden on her daughter. This also fed into her sense of accomplishment and purpose in life.

Her early "morning" dog walks increased to three times a day. During which she was able to socialise with others who were regular dog walkers too. This also had the added benefit of feeling connected to the wider world.

Mindfulness

Octavia really benefitted from learning how to become more mindful in all that she was doing. It also proved to be extremely beneficially in learning how to regulate her emotions by using the metaphor of "surfing the waves" of life and how "bad" times are always only temporary.

Octavia had spent much of her emotional energy re-living past events, so mindfulness was extremely helpful to her in learning to live in the present moment and to focus her attention on what she was engaging with. She learned also to acknowledge her thoughts in a non-judgmental way and to refocus her attention, with practice. She particularly benefitted from, and enjoyed, learning mindful laughter.

She was taught relaxation and meditation techniques to accompany her understanding of how mindfulness can really help with focused attention in the present moment.

Invest in Self

This began with Octavia's need to feel "worthy" of self-care. Starting with her physical appearance, which she had highlighted as a particular need, Octavia began by building in more self-nurture into her daily routine. This included wearing her favourite clothes, applying her make up, wearing her scent, using nice bathing products, and dyeing her hair once again. She was encouraged to keep this (even if no one would "see" her) as it was vital for her to see how investing in herself would lead to an increased positive mood. Self-love and nurture are crucial components in investing in self (especially for those like Octavia who have endured adverse childhood experiences and who may not feel "worthy").

As Octavia's mood improved, she gradually returned to her self-employed role as a delivery driver. Prior to Lockdown, Octavia felt as though she was "existing" in her current job. However, when she completed the "My True Vocation" activity it came up that there were actually lots of really positive things she was enjoying about her work as a delivery driver, but she had always (even as a child) wanted to work delivering the morning post (to be a "Post-woman" as she described it). It transpired that the things she disliked most about her role as a delivery driver were being self-employed, long hours and working to tight delivery deadlines (together with unpredictable pay). So, moving forward Octavia agreed to set herself the long-term goal of investing in how to research jobs in the postal delivery service that were not self-employed. This instilled a sense of hope in the future.

Invest in Others

Octavia became aware of the need of investing in others and the importance of both kindness and radical forgiveness of those who had mistreated her in her past. She found the concept of post traumatic growth (PTG) especially helpful. Also, how forgiveness can be essential in helping to set her free in order to progress in her life going forward.

Her daughter was the most important person in her life and the one on whom she wanted to forge a stronger bond with. So, Octavia began to set time aside each week to do a different and enjoyable activity together. These ranged from trips out, picnics (especially in nature and at the beach), movie nights in and "special teas" in!

Together with building stronger bonds with her daughter, Octavia was keen to extend her own social circle. She started to rekindle old friendships by meeting up for regular coffee dates, and by taking up the offers (and by offering herself too) of any social gatherings from her "new" dog walking friends.

Nature

Octavia's daily walks with her dog were a crucial way of helping her to become more mindful within nature. The fact that Octavia was outside with her dog at different times of the day (mostly early morning and evening) she was enjoying noticing the changing facets of nature which appear at those times. She was enjoying listening to the birds singing first thing each morning on her walks, how the sun cast its shadows upon rising, the smells and sounds of the natural world at different places on her walks. She was loving how in the evenings the sounds, smells and sights around her differed to those of her morning dog walks. She found that she now paid attention to (and enjoyed) different weather together with the changing seasons. In short Octavia had gained a greater awareness, appreciation, and sense of connectedness with the wider natural world around her. All these things impacted positively on her mood and sense of wellbeing.

Diet

At first, Octavia had lost interest in food as her mood had significantly influenced her appetite. The food she was eating was not nourishing her mind, body, or her soul.

Octavia really benefited from mindful eating, by learning how to savour her food again. She needed to believe that she worthy of eating wholesome nourishing and tasty food. She found applying the principles of dining "Like Royalty" extremely helpful in terms of making each meal an "occasion" and by using her "finest" crockery, she was indeed treating herself (and her daughter) like they were deserving of the "best."

As Octavia's mood and activity levels increased, and she established a regular sleep routine, she found her appetite improved. She also began to take responsibility for the preparation of the meals for both her and her daughter. In doing so, and by having a greater understanding of the impact of diet on emotional and physical wellbeing, Octavia found that her motivation and interest to cook healthy meals from scratch increased.

She also began to enjoy the social side of eating again too, both with her daughter and her wider, extended social circle too.

Affirmations

Affirmations became an integral part of Octavia's daily routine, both in her recovery and her ongoing life. Many of the affirmations were directed towards being loved, worthy, kind, grateful, and forgiving. In doing so, she was able to create a more motivated, compassionate, and hopeful mindset going forward into the future too.

Octavia – What Happened Next?

Octavia continues to build the REMIND components into her everyday life. She also feels that she has "come a long way" in her personal recovery and now has the strong belief that she is "deserving" of a good and happy life.

Her relationship with her daughter is extremely strong. She is due to start university soon – Octavia is extremely proud of her.

She continues to walk her dog each day and has recently joined a walking group with other dog walkers where she continues to make new friends, socialise, and experience lots of new adventures in nature.

Although she had the long-term goal of becoming a "post woman", she now has a new job, which she landed "by chance" (through one of her dog walking friends). Octavia has recently started a new daily position delivering hot midday meals to the local schools and care homes in her area. She is loving her new challenge and is on a permanent paid contract with her local authority, where she meets and works with people who value her. She has a restored purpose and meaning to her life. She has regained her sense of hope.

A Final REMIND-er

I hope you have found this book helpful, and that, the case studies throughout have demonstrated how easy and effective the REMIND approach is in changing your life.

Try to incorporate each of the elements of the REMIND approach into your life right now.

REMIND yourself that you are worthy of investment. You deserve to be happy and to fulfil your potential in life. Age should never be a barrier in finding your true vocation in life or in fulfilling your potential. You deserve to be happy and to succeed. There will never be another you. You are unique with unique gifts to give to the world. Now go out and find the happiness, success, and fulfilment you deserve in life.

Good luck.

Chapter 9
Asking for Help

Sometimes you may need to reach out and ask for help. Remember it is okay not to be okay. It is also okay to ask for help too when you need it. You do not have to reach "crisis" point. You are worthy of help, and everyone benefits from support from time to time.

It takes great courage to admit you need help and to seek it. Do not struggle on alone ever, support is always available, and it might just change your life.

If you are struggling and need help it is always advisable to speak directly to your family doctor (GP) who can refer you to sources of support on the NHS in the UK.

If you are seeking a private psychotherapist or counsellor, it is vital to firstly check out their qualifications, credentials, background and most importantly to see if you connect with them. Remember that when entering a therapeutic relationship, you need to have good rapport with your therapist so that you can get the most out of your therapy. So always do your research first and do not just contact the first person you see on a list (even if they charge less). Take your time. If you can, go on personal recommendations. You may know someone who has gone through therapy who can recommend a good fit for you. Many therapists do not include "testimonials" on their websites due to confidentiality issues so do your homework and find out as much as you can about the professional person, in whom you will be trusting your inner most thoughts.

I have provided some useful sources of help and support below for both the UK and those who live beyond in other countries too.

United Kingdom:
Samaritans.
https://www.samaritans.org/
Telephone free: 116 123 (24 hours a day)
Email: jo@samaritans.org
This is a UK based charity which provides a free listening service in a confidential and non-judgmental way to those in crisis.

Saneline.
http://www.sane.org.uk/what_we_do/support/helpline
Telephone free: 0300 304 7000 (4.30 to 10.30 pm each day)
This is a UK based charity which offers a national out of hours helpline for anyone experiencing a mental health problem, or for those who may be caring or supporting someone who is.

Every Mind Matters NHS
https://www.nhs.uk/every-mind-matters/
Lots of helpful advice in the UK on mental health and wellbeing.

Mind.

https://www.mind.org.uk/

UK based charity which provides lots of helpful details around mental health and sources of support.

Anxiety UK.

https://www.anxietyuk.org.uk/

UK based charity helping people experiencing anxiety.

Private Help.

If you want to get help privately, there is always a fee which you will need to pay (sometimes you can claim this back if you have private health insurance). Paying privately means you may be able to get an appointment sooner than on the NHS.

National Council of Integrative Psychotherapists:

https://www.the-ncip.org/ This is one of the oldest professional organisations in the UK for qualified and integrative psychotherapists. If you are looking for a private therapist or counsellor, the NCIP has a professional register where you can find a practitioner local to you. Many of the practitioners are trained in a range of different approaches rather than just one. This means that if you are searching for a more "holistic" approach to therapy, the NCIP may be the best place to search.

UK Databases of Private Therapists and Counsellors:

Psychology Today.

https://www.psychologytoday.com/gb/counselling

Counselling Directory.

https://www.counselling-directory.org.uk/

National Council of Integrative Psychotherapists

https://www.the-ncip.org/

International Sources of Support.

Befrienders Worldwide.

https://www.befrienders.org/

This is an international charity to help anyone in emotional crisis. Their volunteers and members aim to help anyone experiencing emotional crisis or distress (or those close to them) around the world with confidential support.

International Private Help:

Psychology Today.

https://www.psychologytoday.com/intl/counsellors?d omain=content&cc=gb&cl=en

If you are searching internationally then Psychology Today is a global database of fully qualified therapists and counsellors in your own country/ territory.

Bibliography

Armitage, M. (2016) Play is a Child's Work – or is it? Available at: https://www.marc-armitage.com/blog-archive/play-is-a-childs-work-or-is-it_111s44.

Bergin B., Amaladoss N,. Amaladoss A. (2020) How to effectively prescribe exercise. Psychiatric Time. Available at: https://www.psychiatrictimes.com/view/how-to-effectively-prescribe-exercise.

Campbell A. (2022) Cover star Bradley Wiggins reflects on a turbulent ten year ride. Men's Health. Available at: https://www.menshealth.com/uk/mental-strength/a39726563/cover-star-bradley-wiggins/

Doran, G. T. (1981). There's a S.M.A.R.T. Way to Write Management's Goals and Objectives. Management Review, 70, 35–36.

Fisher, A (2020) A daily routine for managing depression and chronic pain. Healthline. Available at:

https://www.healthline.com/health/mental-health/daily-quarantine-routine-for-depression-chronic-pain.

Grenville-Cleave, B. Boniwell, I. (2019) Live Happy, 100 simple ways to fill your life with joy. London. Modern Books.

Gotschi T., Garrard J., Giles-Corti B. (2016) Cycling as a Part of Daily Life: A review of Health Benefits. Transport Reviews. Vol36 (1). Available at:
https://www.tandfonline.com/doi/full/10.1080/01441647.20 15.1057877

Iljon Foreman E, Pollard C (2016) CBT Your Toolkit to Modify Mood Overcome Obstructions and Improve Your Life. London. Icon Books.

Kabat-Zinn, J. (2019) Wherever You Go, There You Are. Mindfulness Meditation for Everyday Life. London. Piatkus.

Kapoor A. (2021) Can laughter beat depression? Calm Sage. Available at:
https://www.calmsage.com/can-laughter-therapy-beat-depression/

Kataria M. (2020) Laughter Yoga – Daily Practices for Health and Happiness. London. Yellow Kite: Hodder and Stoughton Ltd.

Lu P., Oh J., Leahy K.E., Chopik W. J. (2021) Friendship importance around the World: Links to cultural factors, health and well-being. Frontiers in Psychology. Available at:

https://www.frontiersin.org/articles/10.3389/fpsyg.2020.570839/full

McMains S., Kastner S. (2011). Interactions of top-down and bottom-up mechanisms in human visual cortex. Journal of Neuroscience. 31 (2) p587–597.

Mental Health Foundation (2021). Diet and Mental Health. Available at: https://www.mentalhealth.org.uk/a-to-z/d/diet-and-mental-health

Mental Health Foundation (ND). Nature: How connecting with nature benefits our mental health. Available at: https://www.mentalhealth.org.uk/campaigns/nature/nature-research

Mind (2021) Food and Mood. Available at: https://www.mind.org.uk/information-support/tips-for-everyday-living/food-and-mood/about-food-and-mood/

Mind (2018) Nature and Mental Health. Available at: https://www.mind.org.uk/information-support/tips-for-everyday-living/nature-and-mental-health/how-nature-benefits-mental-health/

Moore N. (2017) Mindful Thoughts for Cyclists, Finding Balance on Two Wheels. Brighton. Leaping Hare Press.

Monda L. (2000) The Practice of Wholeness: Spiritual Transformation in Everyday Life. Golden Flower Publications.

Nadler R. T., Rabi R., Minda J. P. (2010) Better Mood and Better Performance: Learning Rule – Described Categories is Enhanced by Positive Mood. Psychological Science. Vol 21 (12) p 1770–1776.

Poole H. (ND) Who discovered the Law of Attraction: Uncovering the truth. Available at:
https://manifestwithease.com/who-discovered-law-of-attraction/

Raines A. M., Boffa J. W., Allan N. P., Short N. A., Schmidt N. B. (2015) Hoarding and eating pathology: The mediating role of emotion regulation. Comprehensive Psychiatry. (57) p 29–35.

Random Acts of Kindness Foundation. Available at:
https://www.randomactsofkindness.org/

Robinson L, Segal J, Smith M (2021). The Mental Health Benefits of Exercise. Available at:
https://www.helpguide.org/articles/healthy-living/the-mental-health-benefits-of-exercise.htm

Saxbe D. E., Repetti R. (2009). No place like home: Home tours correlate with daily patterns of mood and cortisol. Personality and social psychology bulletin. Available at:
https://journals.sagepub.com/doi/abs/10.1177/0146167209352864 ityad Social Psychology Bulletin Pty and Social Psychology Bulletin.

Seligman M. E. P. (2012). Flourish: A Visionary New Understanding of Happiness and Wellbeing. Simon and Schuster.

Spielman A.J., Saskin P., Thorpy M. J. (1987). Treatment of chronic insomnia by restriction of time in bed. Sleep. 10(1) 45–56. Available at:
https://pubmed.ncbi.nlm.nih.gov/3563247/

Telloian, C (2019) 11 Tips for a morning routine that supports mental health. Good Therapy. Available at:
https://www.goodtherapy.org/blog/11-tips-for-a-morning-routine-that-supports-mental-health-1022197

Titmus, C. (2014) Mindfulness for Everyday Living. London. Octopus Publishing Group.

Toussaint, L., Shields G. S., Dorn G., Slavich G. M. (2016) Effects of lifetime stress exposure on mental and physical health in young adulthood: How stress degrades and forgiveness protects health. Journal of Health Psychology. Available at:
https://journals.sagepub.com/doi/10.1177/135910531454413 2?url_ver=Z39.88-2003&rfr_id=ori:rid:crossref.org&rfr_dat=cr_pub%3dpubm ed

Withey, J (2020) How to Tell Depression to Piss Off. 40 Ways to Get your Life Back. London. Little Brown Book Group.

Tedeschi R. G., & Calhoun L. G. (1996). The Posttraumatic Growth Inventory: Measuring the positive legacy of trauma. Journal of Traumatic Stress, 9, 455–472.

Tedeschi R. G, Cann A., Taku K., Senol-Durak., E., Calhoun L G. (2017). The Posttraumatic Growth Inventory: A Revision Integrating Existential and Spiritual Change. Journal of Traumatic Stress, 30, 11–18

The Guardian (2020). Doctors to prescribe bike rides to tackle UK obesity crisis. Available at:
https://www.theguardian.com/politics/2020/jul/26/doctors-to-prescribe-bike-rides-to-tackle-uk-obesity-crisis-amid-coronavirus-risk

UK-Rehab (2021) Shopping addiction explained. Available at:
https://www.uk-rehab.com/behavioural-addictions/shopping/

Ventiglio A., Sancassiani F., Contu M. P., Latorre M., Di Slavatore M., Fornaro M., Bhugra D. (2020). Mediterranean Diet and its benefits on Health and Mental Health: A literature review. Clinical Practice and Epidemiology in Mental Health. Available at:
https://www.ncbi.nlm.nih.gov/pmc/articles/PMC7536728/

White M., Alcock I., Grellier J., Wheeler B. W., Hartig T., Warber S. L., Bone A., Depledge M. H., Fleming L. E. (2019). Spending at least 120 minutes a week in nature is associated with good health and wellbeing. Scientific Reports. Vol 9,

7730. Available at: https://www.nature.com/articles/s41598-019-44097-3

Weir K. (2017) Forgiveness can improve mental and physical health. CE Corner. American Psychological Association. Available at: https://www.apa.org/monitor/2017/01/ce-corner

World Health Organisation (WHO) (2020) Physical Activity. Available at:
https://www.who.int/news-room/fact-sheets/detail/physical-activity

Yoshikawa Y., Ohmaki E., Kawahata H., Meakawa Y., Ogihara Y., Morishita R., Aok M. (2019). Beneficial effect of laughter therapy on physiological and psychological function in elders. Nursing Open. 6(1): 93–99. Available at: https://www.ncbi.nlm.nih.gov/pmc/articles/PMC6279721/